The
Game Cookbook

The Game Cookbook

Geraldine Steindler

Stoeger Publishing Company

Published by the Stoeger Publishing Company,
55 Ruta Court, South Hackensack, New Jersey 07606

Twelfth printing, May 1983

ISBN: 0-88317-000-0

Manufactured in the United States of America

Distributed to the book trade and to the
sporting goods trade by Stoeger Industries,
55 Ruta Court, South Hackensack, New Jersey 07606

In Canada, distributed to the book trade and to the
sporting goods trade by Stoeger Canada, Ltd.,
165 Idema Road, Markham, Ontario L3R 1A9

To a cook's greatest inspiration —
good trenchermen — and most particularly
to those who have graced our table

THANKS TO

Don Frevert — for his excellent drawings

That Fine Old Gent Popowski — for his gems of wisdom during our memorable hunt with him last year

Chris Klineburger — although he never did tell me exactly how to make Eskimo ice cream

Mrs. G. C. F. Dalziel and The Whitehorse Star — for her Northern specialties

My Mother and Dad — for suffering through my earliest attempts in the kitchen and teaching me pride in culinary skill

My Mother-in-law — for introducing me to a whole new world of cooking — the Viennese way

My husband — who has suffered with me the "birthing" of this book — and my cooking — and lived to tell the tale!

Contents

PREFACE

As I LOOK BACK ON IT, this book has been a-borning for many years—ever since my husband introduced me to guns and the pleasures of the hunt. Just an ordinary housewife with no special training, but with a love of good food, I began to search for new and different ways to prepare the game we brought home. Since general cook books usually devote but a page or two to game cooking, I began to experiment on my own. I became what my husband calls "a substitute cook"—substituting ingredients on hand for those listed in a recipe. It soon became a family joke at the dinner table—"Well, what recipe did you change today?"

As my interest in game cooking developed, and the quantity and variety of game increased, my search for recipes widened. A casual word in conversation with other hunters and their wives, an effort to reproduce a special dish enjoyed in a restaurant, a search for old family recipes dimly remembered from childhood—all these brought needed diversity and fresh interest. Like any oft-repeated job, cooking can become monotonous and boring — for the cook as well as the diners.

I was persuaded to write things down, so that particularly successful "experiments" might be repeated. Gradually my jumble of notes evolved into a card file of sorts.

It might never have progressed beyond this stage had I not become aware that the game we enjoyed so much had fallen into disrepute with many people. Two statements I have heard so often the last few years finally goaded me into action: "It's so gamey—I don't like it!" "But it needs so much preparation—all those complicated recipes!"

Like anything else, game cooking can be as simple or as complicated as you care to make it. Game, properly taken care of, still provides the finest of gourmet dining, whether you're squatting beside a campfire or seated at a candle-lit, damask-covered table.

This book is written primarily for those, like myself, who have not grown up in the wilds, but who do like to escape into the woods and fields with dog and gun and who would like to enjoy the fruits of the hunt at the dinner table. A few of the recipes are frankly fancy for those special occasions; ⚘ designates those recipes suitable for camp cooking, requiring only those basic ingredients found in camp kitchens or in trail packs.

I hope you will use this book as a point of departure for your own adventures in the kitchen and over the campfire. Change it, adapt it, season it with your own imagination and ingenuity, but always serve game with pride—it can't be surpassed!

GERALDINE STEINDLER
Libertyville, Illinois

July, 1964

The
Game Cookbook

CHAPTER I

Don't Blame The Game!

(OR THE COOK, EITHER!)

EVERY YEAR MORE PEOPLE are turning to the woods and fields with shotgun and rifle for relaxation and pleasure. For many of us, hunting has become a delightful escape from the pressures of modern living. It should follow that we have a wider interest in game on the dining table, but from my experience, it just ain't so!

When the conversation turns to hunting and we confess our honest preference for game over "store bought" meat, the expressions range from disbelief to ill-concealed sympathy for the poor wife who has to cook that "gamey" stuff her husband brings home. Often we have received game from crestfallen hunters whose wives wouldn't—or didn't know how to—cook it. Our offers of game to acquaintances have on occasion been refused or, at best, accepted with great reservations.

It wasn't always this way. The early settlers of this country depended on the bountiful wild game for their very existence. While it was everyday fare for the backwoodsman, game also graced the most festive tables in Colonial Williamsburg. In Victorian days, the market hunters ravaged the herds and flocks to satisfy the ever-increasing demands of connoisseurs of that elegant—and often overstuffed—era of dining.

There are still many people in the more sparsely settled regions of this country who rely on their skill with the gun for their winter meat. However, for the great majority of us who are only five or ten minutes away from a supermarket, the situation is quite different. When you are accustomed to neatly wrapped packages of roasts and chops from the meat counter, it can be a bewildering experience to be confronted with several hundred pounds of meat on the hoof! This is where the trouble begins! The "gaminess" so often objected to is simply spoiled or tainted meat, caused by neglect or lack of knowledge on the hunter's part.

It is true that an animal's diet does affect the flavor of the meat. A bear feeding on carrion or prowling the garbage dumps certainly cannot be compared with one grown fat on nuts and berries, and there will naturally be a vast difference in flavor between ducks feeding on fish and those feeding on wild celery. The mating season also affects the flavor and texture of the meat of large game animals—unfavorably so! However, these elements of chance are part and parcel of the hunting game. What *is* distressing is the fact that too many pounds of superb meat are wasted each year by conditions over which the hunter *does* have control.

No cook worthy of her salt should be expected to work miracles in the kitchen with improperly cared-for game—as a matter of fact, it's impossible! Therefore, as a part-time hunter as well as a full-time cook, I shall venture away from the pots and pans long enough for a discussion of those all-important procedures before the cook takes over.

PLAN AHEAD

Caring for game actually begins before you leave home for your hunting trip, whether it be three weeks in a mountain wilderness or a morning's stroll through a nearby shooting preserve. Guns, boots, camping gear, hunter—all set and raring to go! But what about the game you're going to bring home? Oh sure, your well sharpened hunting knife is on your belt—but do you have a pocket stone to *keep* it sharp? If you're not going with a guide, what about a hatchet for quartering that bull moose or trophy sized deer? It may be a long trek back to your hunting vehicle after your noble prize is down, and quartering the beast on the spot may be your only way of getting it out. A few good sized, heavy weight plastic sacks take no space at all in a pocket of your hunting coat and are mighty handy for bringing out the treasured heart and liver. Of course, you don't mind a bit of blood on your hunting coat, but it doesn't do the liver much good to be associated with the debris that always collects in game pockets.

Large sacks made of lightweight canvas (or even sturdy muslin bed sheets) are invaluable for keeping dust and flies from the meat. Cheesecloth, frequently suggested for this purpose, is practically useless in rough country—it tears readily and does not really keep out the dust. Our meat sacks are 5 ft. long and 3 ft. wide, large enough to accommodate a fair sized critter without struggle. Figure 2 yds. of 72 in. lightweight canvas or unbleached cotton duck per sack. Make a double fold of material on each seam, stitch each seam twice with heavy duty thread, and provide a sturdy drawstring at the top. It doesn't take long to whip them up on the sewing machine and they can be washed and reused for years.

Even an hour's drive to a shooting preserve calls for a bit of advance preparation. When we were training our young springer pup, we always took along a portable cooler with a few cans of Scotch Ice on our jaunts to the preserve. Early fall days can be mighty warm in most parts of the country, and that cooler prevented many a disastrously parboiled pheasant.

Is this advance preparation "counting your chickens before they're hatched?" Not as far as we are concerned. If we're skunked, so be it. If we connect, we've made sure the game arrives home in edible condition.

THE GUN AND THE SHOT

Far be it from me to add my voice to the ever-raging controversy over gun calibers. But *do* suit your gun to the game you're after and to the country in which you're hunting. A caliber adequate for a clean kill on elk or moose is just too much for a pronghorn. Likewise, a flat shooting rifle capable of downing an antelope at 300 yards in open country is of little use in the heavy brush of the Maine woods.

Use a caliber of rifle and a bullet weight sufficient to kill quickly and cleanly. A wounded and frightened animal that runs is usually so full of adrenalin that you might just as well bury the meat and chew on the hide, once you have tracked him down and ended his suffering. On the other hand, too large a caliber or too heavy a bullet for the job at hand will cause extensive meat damage. Even a well placed lung shot in this situation may cause so much internal damage that the visceral cavity is punctured by bone fragments.

I think most hunters will agree that a well placed shot just behind the shoulder will down an animal effectively with little meat damage. A brain or neck shot is not only more difficult because of the small lethal area involved, but it may ruin a lovely head. A spinal shot is certainly a disabling one, but don't plan on too many chops from your animal in this case. A shot in the mid section is to be avoided if at all possible—it may be fatal, but it certainly is messy and the chances are excellent that the meat will be tainted by the spillage from the viscera.

FIELD DRESSING

Big Game

As soon as your animal is down—and do make certain it is actually dead and not just stunned—get the photographs taken in a hurry and then roll up your sleeves. You have a job ahead of you that should be accomplished without delay! Since the body heat of the animal encourages bacterial decay, it is important to remove the innards and allow the carcass to cool as quickly as possible.

Decide now whether or not you wish to have a head mount as some of your cuts in the field dressing will vary as you proceed. Then too, greater care must be taken to keep the head and cape hair free from blood if it is to adorn your den wall at some future date.

Exactly how you proceed with the field dressing is a matter of individual preference. Six experienced hunters will give you six slightly different approaches to the matter. The subject has been thoroughly discussed in books and magazines countless times, complete with diagrams. Several points do bear repetition, however, if you would bring home prime meat.

If the animal has scent glands, and you choose to remove these first, be certain that all taint from these areas is *completely* scrubbed from hands as well as knife before you make any further incisions.

Although the field dressing should be done with dispatch, especially if the weather is unseasonably warm, do proceed with caution. One hasty slash of the knife can spill the contents of the stomach, bladder or intestines into the body cavity and create just the sort of damage you so carefully avoided with your well placed shot.

Once the innards have been removed, rescue the heart and liver. Remove the gall bladder from the liver without puncturing it, if one is present, by slicing out a small section of the liver along with it. Put the heart and liver in the plastic sack you carried along, slosh them around with water to remove the excess blood, then drain and set aside.

One source of spoiled meat has been removed with the innards, but you still have a few minutes' work on the carcass. If the animal is not on an incline with the head uphill, place it so. Spread the cavity wide, and scrub thoroughly with water to remove the blood and any body fluids that remain. Pay particular attention to the wound area. I shall probably be accused of rank heresy over this statement, but water, if at all available, is much preferable to grass or your handkerchief and is more efficient. Wipe the cavity dry and turn the animal upside down over a fence, a bush, or downed timber—or hang it from a tree, head up—any method convenient under the circumstances to complete the drainage. To hasten the cooling process, keep the body cavity spread wide to allow a good circulation of air.

While you light a cigarette and contemplate your next move, let me toss in a suggestion. Although most hunters of our acquaintance don't bother with it, those who live entirely on game would not consider discarding the tongue of the antlered game—it is equally as delicious as beef tongue. Especially if you are not planning on a full head mount, remove the tongue, leaving on the skin and roots. A large moose tongue can be the basis of several delicious camp meals and has the same advantage as liver and heart—you can cook and eat it the same day it was removed from the animal.

Your next move depends entirely on where you are and how warm it is. If it's a long hike back to camp or your hunting vehicle and you have an elk or moose to cope with, skinning the animal on the spot and then quartering it would be most advantageous. This permits more rapid cooling of the meat, so essential with the larger animals. The quarters can then be packed out in the meat sacks you brought along. If you are alone, the sacked quarters should be hung in trees or raised off the ground in some fashion for air circulation until you can return with help.

If a deer must be transported any distance through the woods, the hide is best left on to protect the meat in the dragging or carrying process. Since deer are smaller, they do cool more rapidly than their larger cousins, and removing the hide can safely wait to be done in camp where it's more convenient. In rain or snow, the hide affords protection, especially if circumstances force you to hang your deer for a few days. Hang the deer head up for two reasons: drainage of fluid is better and rain or snow will run off the hide with the direction of the hair.

The picture changes drastically, of course, if the weather is warm. Get that hide off as fast as possible, hang in an airy place and then protect the meat from blow flies, dust and magpies with the meat sack drawn over the hanging carcass. No matter when you skin the carcass, trim away, right then and there, all bone splinters and every trace of blood shot tissue.

Antelope are handled in much the same way as deer. Since it is usually warm during antelope season, the animal should be skinned just as soon as it has been hog dressed. It is then hustled into a meat sack to protect it against the clouds of alkali dust and the swarms of flies that seem to appear from nowhere as soon as you start cutting.

Particular care should be taken during the entire operation not to touch the scent patches as you work and thus taint the meat. These patches will come off with the hide. To keep the brittle hairs from breaking off and spreading to the meat, roll the hide hair side under as you skin.

Hanging game to age or season it is another subject of controversy. *If* the weather is dry, *if* the temperature is about 30°-40° and *if* it can be depended on not to fluctuate too much either way, fine and dandy— hang your game! But be sure it's hung away from predators. Since all these ideal conditions for proper hanging and aging are seldom found outside a butcher's cold room, it has been generally conceded that the sure way to preserve that wonderful meat in its most flavorful condition is to skin it as quickly as possible, cool it rapidly and freeze it without delay. I agree that freezing will not make a prime filet mignon out of a bull elk shoulder roast but then, neither will any amount of hanging. Rapid processing and freezing does, however, insure that the meat will suffer no further deterioration. Some professional butchers have stated in recent years that quick-freezing will accomplish the same tenderizing process as several weeks of hanging.

At the risk of sounding repetitious, I shall state once more what has been said by others thousands of times. It is still unheeded, so obviously needs repeating. DON'T display that unskinned carcass on the top of your car or draped over the radiator. You're only displaying your ignorance, not your prowess as a hunter.

On our trip West last year, we saw numerous animals transported thus. From the license plates, we knew these hunters had at least 12-18 hours' drive in 90°-100° weather before that meat could be processed. Gas station attendants, waitresses in diners, scores of local people talked with us about it. The comment heard over and over was "We like to see the hunters come, we like to see them get their game, but what a pity to see all that meat ruined! No wonder some folks say they don't like game—that meat is spoiled already!"

FIELD DRESSING

Birds

The very same principles apply to birds as to large game. Draw— remove crop and intestines—as soon after shooting as possible. The shot pellets can, and very often do, penetrate the internal organs, allowing seepage of the digestive juices and partially digested food into the flesh. In this way, you eliminate to a very large extent the fishy flavor of ducks and geese, and the bitter taste found in some grouse.

Dry-pluck the birds in the field as soon as feasible by pulling the feathers downward in the direction they grow. It is much easier to remove the feathers while the birds are still warm and there is also less danger of tearing the skin. (Your wife will also appreciate the lack of feathers in the basement.)

Clean the body cavity and transport the cleaned birds home in a well-iced portable cooler. The final removal of pinfeathers, plus any shot pellets that have penetrated the skin, can be done at home. Store cleaned birds, loosely covered with waxed paper, in the refrigerator for a few days before cooking—or package carefully and freeze. It is a wise idea to mark the packages accordingly if the birds have been badly damaged and would not be attractive for broiling or roasting.

Many of the old recipes call for hanging a bird, either plucked or in plumage, for several days to a week. This, of course, was before the days of central heating and a cool dry spot wasn't too hard to find. The same effect may be obtained by refrigerator storage at 45°.

One final word: if you have older pheasants in your game bag (indicated by long, sharp claws) save time by skinning them, since they'll not be roasted anyhow. Cut off the feet and the first wing joints and unzip them from their overcoats—the shot pellets which have lodged just under the skin will go along with it.

FIELD DRESSING

Small Game

The smaller game animals are drawn, skinned and cleaned, and then stored in the same manner as birds. There are two precautions to be observed, however. Rabbits and opossums are both subject to tularemia. When hunting, beware of the sluggish rabbit, which may be infected with this disease. When cleaning and skinning these animals, either wear gloves or scrub your hands thoroughly *immediately* afterwards, lest you become infected by the germ entering the bloodstream through a cut or scratch on your hand. If you discover a spotted liver as you draw a rabbit, proceed no further—just bury the critter then and there.

All of the smaller game animals except squirrel and porcupine have scent glands under the skin, along the spine and under the forelegs. The muskrat has an additional pair located in the pelvic region. Care should be taken when skinning not to cut these glands as they are removed.

Strip as much fat as possible from porcupine, opossum, raccoon, woodchuck and beaver before storing in refrigerator or packaging and freezing.

LOCKER PREPARATION

The larger animals—bear, boar, and the antlered game—still have to be translated into the more familiar roasts and chops—and here you have several choices.

In many game areas, freezer locker plants will do the entire job of cutting to your specifications, packaging and quick freezing at a reasonable cost. If you tell them beforehand when you plan to pick up your processed meat, in many instances they will have dry ice and insulated cartons available to insure your precious cargo on the trip home. Keep in mind, however, the fact that this is an extremely busy season for these people. They may not have the man power or the freezing facilities to do an overnight job for you.

If you have a reliable butcher at home, by all means make use of his speed and skill, as well as his familiarity with your preferences. But be certain *before* you leave on your hunt that he will tackle the job. Many butchers and locker plant owners in urban areas flatly refuse to handle game, or else charge excessive rates for processing to discourage the requests. We have asked quite a number of them why and the answer is an additional reason for the necessity of this chapter. In the past, they have handled game that was tainted or improperly cared for in some fashion and found that the odors permeated domestic meats hanging in the same cooler. There certainly could be no objection, though, if you bring in an animal that has been properly dressed and cooled, and *kept* cool with dry ice on the trip home.

Regardless of who does the butchering, be sure that all possible fat is removed from the meat, as this fat is the final contributor to the objectionable "gaminess" and its "off" flavor permeates the meat even in the freezer. An additional check for blood clots and damaged tissue to be removed should be made during the butchering. If your family is not overly fond of 'burgers, have the rib sections prepared for barbecueing and enjoy the added bonus of flank steaks. When you do have 'burgers ground, stress the fact that beef suet be substituted for the game fat in whatever proportion you desire. At least a small amount of fat is essential for juicy 'burgers. Some old-timers, and they are indeed rare jewels, will even prepare sausage for you with their own jealously guarded herb blends.

Specify the thickness of steaks and chops—there's nothing more disappointing to a lover of rare meat than a paper thin chop or steak. (And venison chops *are* most tender and flavorful when cooked rare.) If you have a small family, order a few choice roasts cut to serve a larger number of people on gala occasions. One of our favorite stunts is to have the tenderloins removed whole, to be sliced as needed for filet mignons of the desired thickness. You might also consider a crown roast of venison, made of 12 ribs—a truly noble feast in the grand manner.

You may get a raised eyebrow from the butcher on this next suggestion, but it is a good one. Ask him to collect all the bones in one or two packages. (see Chap. II) Perhaps you can persuade him to bone and tie some of the roasts. Boned meat takes much less freezer space and there is less danger of the wrapping being punctured. If you have not already eaten all the heart and liver, it too can be packaged and frozen.

Request that freezer wrapper paper with a plastic coating be used (never butcher paper), that the packages be double wrapped and clearly marked as to the specific cut of meat.

You can, of course, do the job yourself. It is not as difficult as some would have you believe—and I speak from experience! I might never have had the courage to volunteer for the job, but circumstances forced me into it last year and I shall not hesitate to tackle it again.

My husband shot a mule deer the last day of our hunt and we brought it home skinned and quartered, along with two antelope that had been cut, packaged and frozen at a locker plant in our hunting territory. Knowing that we would be on the road for 36 hours, we packed all the meat in a large wooden box, added 40 pounds of dry ice and insulated the box with our sleeping bags. After my husband left for his office the next morning, I brought a good sturdy table into the kitchen and armed myself with a sharp knife, a meat saw and a cleaver. With a diagram of beef cuts from a cookbook to guide me, and a box of Band-aids within easy reach, I set to work.

Quartering, in my opinion, is strictly man's work, if only to suspend the animal by its hind legs. If you can work in a garage or screened porch, I recommend it. Drive two sturdy spikes in an overhead beam and hang the carcass with meat hooks placed in the slits between the Achilles tendons and the bones of the hind legs. If you *must* work outside, tie a stout rope through each slit you have made and hoist away over a sturdy tree branch. Be sure the carcass is securely anchored and evenly balanced, for you will be exerting a fair amount of pressure on an already weighty object.

Your first job is to remove the neck by cutting at right angles to the backbone ahead of the shoulder blade. Then open up the carcass completely by splitting, with hatchet or cleaver, the breast bone and the pelvis right down the midline. The carcass is then divided into two halves, either by splitting with a hatchet along one side of the spinal column, or by sawing through the middle of the spinal column. The second method is slower and a bit more difficult, but does produce a neater finished product.

Remove the halves from the hooks or ropes and place them on a sturdy table to quarter them. You might assume that a whole carcass would give you four quarters, but you are now about to produce three quarters from each half—the forequarter, the hindquarter, the rib section. The forequarter is removed by a cut just behind the shoulder blade, the hindquarter is cut directly in front of the pin bone or front part of the pelvic bone. The remainder is the mid section, comprising the ribs and the loin. Wipe each quarter with a damp cloth to remove any hairs or bone chips.

Now we've arrived at the point where I started operations. It is convenient to have a fairly empty refrigerator so the quarters may be kept cool until processed.

Decide, before you begin cutting, whether you want rib roasts or chops from the mid section. Remove the flank or belly meat from the lower part of the loin end—reserve for stew, 'burgers, or flank steak. Remove the lower portion of the ribs, with a saw cut, for spare ribs. What remains should resemble a whole pork loin. Cut it into chops of desired thickness by slicing between the ribs and then severing the backbone with a good whack of the cleaver. Do the same with the loin chops, only there will be no ribs to guide you.

The forequarter will end up as three basic pieces—the shoulder blade section, the leg and the shank. Cut the leg off right below the shoulder joint—with a bit of prodding, you should have no trouble finding it—then cut off the lower portion of the leg where the meat is scanty—the shank. The leg roast can be boned and tied or packaged as is. I prefer to bone the shoulder roast (so I can stuff it) especially if the animal is not too large. However, you may simply cut it in two at right angles to the backbone for blade pot roasts. Your saw will get a good workout here!

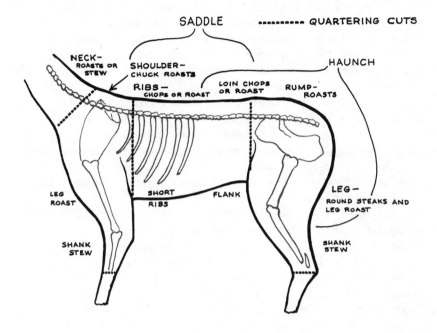

SADDLE   ---------- QUARTERING CUTS

NECK—
ROASTS OR STEW

SHOULDER—
CHUCK ROASTS

HAUNCH

RIBS—
CHOPS OR ROAST

LOIN CHOPS
OR ROAST

RUMP—
ROASTS

LEG
ROAST

SHORT
RIBS

FLANK

LEG—
ROUND STEAKS AND
LEG ROAST

SHANK
STEW

SHANK
STEW

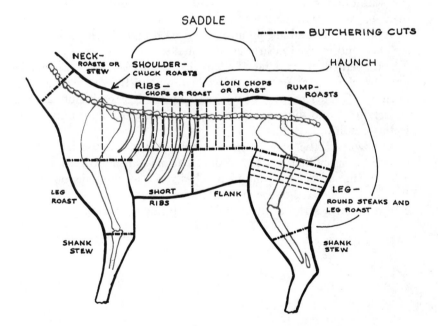

SADDLE   ---·-·-·-· BUTCHERING CUTS

NECK—
ROASTS OR
STEW

SHOULDER—
CHUCK ROASTS

HAUNCH

RIBS—
CHOPS OR ROAST

LOIN CHOPS
OR ROAST

RUMP—
ROASTS

LEG
ROAST

SHORT
RIBS

FLANK

LEG—
ROUND STEAKS AND
LEG ROAST

SHANK
STEW

SHANK
STEW

The hindquarter is divided in similar fashion. The hip section will provide one or two rump roasts, depending on the size of the animal. A cut made just below the point where the hip and leg bones join will separate the rump from the leg or haunch, which furnishes the steaks and roasts. You may prefer to keep one leg whole and cut the other for steaks. When my sawing arm grew tired, I cut each steak to the desired thickness, cut around the leg bone with a thin boning knife and released the steak from the bone. When the size of the steaks began to diminish, I boned out the remainder for a leg roast, again cutting off the scanty portion at the bottom—the shank.

All you have left is the neck section, which can be cut into two portions for pot roasts or trimmed from the bones for stew, 'burgers or mincemeat.

Not being a professional butcher, I found it helpful to take a breather from the cutting and sawing operations and package each quarter as I finished cutting it. I set up wrapping operations on one section of my kitchen counter with scale, freezer paper (one side plastic-coated), plastic film, freezer tape and marking pencil. Freezer paper heavy enough to prevent air seepage—and thus freezer burn— does make a bulky package when you double wrap. Because of its stiffness, it is also hard to exclude all air from awkwardly shaped pieces. I experimented successfully with a thin innner wrapper of the self-adhering plastic film pressed down to exclude all air, and then an outer wrapping of the heavy freezer paper—"drug store" wrapped with a double fold and sealed with tape. Each package was weighed and marked clearly as to contents.

This method of working also enabled me to sharp freeze smaller portions of meat at one time. Overloading the freezer with a large quantity of unfrozen meat is not recommended, since it puts a strain on the motor and the meat is not frozen quickly enough to give satisfactory results.

As I worked, the bones were collected in large plastic bags, to be tended to on another less hectic day. The stew meat was set aside in a large pan and cut into one inch cubes when all else was done. The Band-aids? Yes, I did use one after our beagle jumped too enthusiastically for a scrap of meat and got my finger as well.

CHAPTER II

Soups

WITH THE ACCELERATED PACE of modern living, the old soup kettle has all but disappeared from the kitchen. In its place—a row of cans or a pile of foil envelopes on the pantry shelf. These modern convenience foods are not to be scorned—they are the product of much research, skill and technical know-how—and serve countless purposes in camp or kitchen. However, we are being needlessly wasteful if we never bring the soup kettle out of that far corner of the cupboard. Those bones rescued from the butchering and freezer preparation are an excellent source of nutrition—just ¼ pound of bones yields, with long slow cooking, the same amount of gelatine as two pounds of meat! Furthermore, the stock thus obtained can be used in so many ways—in soups, sauces and casseroles—that it would be a pity to resort to substitutes when the vastly superior ingredient is so easily prepared.

Soup making need not be a time consuming procedure. I consider five or ten minutes extra in the kitchen morning and evening as time well spent for a bank account of good soup to draw upon on those hectic days we all seem to have. While you're tending to breakfast dishes, haul a plastic sack of bones from the freezer and start the stock. By the time the kitchen is squared away, the stock can be skimmed and left to simmer with the vegetables without further attention until dinnertime.

Bones from veal and beef roasts and chops are well worth saving, in addition to those from the larger game animals. Chicken and turkey bones, as well as the carcasses of broiled or roasted game birds, should be collected for white stock. One other "saving" suggestion: when you are planning to serve tongue, ham, or corned beef, be sure you have lentils, beans or split peas on hand. I find it a waste of space to freeze the large amount of liquid in which these meats have been cooked, so I plan to make soup—usually a double batch—by the next day, and then freeze the more concentrated finished product.

I have found it handy to save the waxed paper cartons from cottage cheese for storing stock and completed soups. The one pound cartons are perfect for enough stock for a sauce or gravy recipe, while the two pound size holds almost a full quart of soup. Using these cartons eliminates thawing time, for you just slit the carton and start cooking right away. This is particularly helpful when every minute counts.

If your soup kettle is large enough, by all means double or treble the recipe for any favorite soup. It's definitely a time-saver when you have all the ingredients out anyway and there is only one set of pots to wash!

VENISON STOCK

3 lbs. cracked bones and meat
    trimmings (any antlered
    game)
2 qts. water or vegetable liquid
2 tbsp. salt

Pinch of thyme
Pinch of mace or marjoram
1 tsp. whole peppercorns
2 or 3 bay leaves

4 cups of chopped or sliced vegetables, including the following:
Onion	Mushroom trimmings or
Celery and the leaves	a few dried ones
Carrots	Any leftover vegetables on
Tomatoes, fresh or canned	hand

Part of the bones and meat may be browned first in the oven for a richer color. Using a large kettle with a lid, cover bones and meat with cold water or vegetable liquid and bring to a boil slowly. Skim any foam that rises, add vegetables and seasonings and simmer gently all day (at least 5 hours). Strain through a colander or sieve, cool and remove the fat that forms on top. Package and freeze. Makes about 2 quarts of stock. Bones from roasts and chops may be added to the stated quantity of uncooked bones.

GAME CONSOMME

This is simply clarified stock, which can be served with many attractive garnishes.

To clarify:
1 qt. stock
1 egg white, slightly beaten, plus the crushed egg shell

Combine in a saucepan and heat slowly, stirring constantly. Boil 3 minutes, then simmer slowly for 20 minutes. Skim and strain through cheesecloth.

Serving suggestions:

1. Reheat and garnish with sliced lemon
2. Add 4 tbsp. madeira or dry sherry wine
3. Garnish with custard cubes (see Chap. IX)
4. Garnish with Wiener Erbsen—Viennese peas (see Chap. IX)
5. Add julienne strips of tongue or vegetables
6. Float several Leberknödel—liver dumplings—on each serving (see Chap. IX)
7. Add several game quenelles to each serving (see Chap. IX)
8. Jellied consomme—If original stock has been cooked long enough, consomme will jell when chilled. If not, for 1 quart of stock, add 1 tbsp. unflavored gelatine softened in ½ cup cold consomme and dissolved in hot consomme. Chill—break lightly with fork when serving.
9. If consomme lacks zip, a dash of Worcestershire sauce or lemon juice will do the trick.

MEAT GLAZE

Game bird or venison stock boiled down to jelly stage. This concentrate may be stored in the refrigerator. Use it to add authority to gravy, sauces and stews.

 ONION SOUP

5 or 6 onions, thinly sliced   Dash of Worcestershire sauce
4 tbsps. butter
6 cups venison stock
    (or 6 to 8 bouillon cubes
    and 1½ quarts water)
  Salt and freshly ground
    pepper to taste

Brown the onions slowly in butter and cook over low heat for 15 to 20 minutes. Add venison stock or bouillon, season to taste and simmer an additional 20 minutes. Serve with toasted bread slices sprinkled with Parmesan cheese floating on each bowl.

MUSHROOM CONSOMME

Perfect for a festive game dinner.

2 quarts stock (venison or   Salt to taste
   pheasant)   4 tbsps. butter
3 cups coarsely chopped fresh   2 sprigs parsley
   mushrooms or 2 oz. dried
   mushrooms
3 stalks celery, chopped
1 medium onion, chopped
   A few peppercorns

Brown mushrooms, onion and celery in butter. Add stock, seasonings and parsley. Simmer 1 hour. Strain through a fine sieve or cheesecloth, pressing to extract the liquid from the vegetables. Add ¼ cup sauterne, reheat until piping hot, but do not boil.

BORSHT

This national dish of the Russians and Poles has more variations than the spelling of its name. It may be served hot or cold, strained or as a thick soup, garnished with sour cream or not—but always served with dark rye bread. This basic recipe may be varied according to the ingredients you have on hand. It freezes well, so double the quantities if you wish.

1 quart venison stock
1 cup peeled and shredded beets
3 cups shredded or finely chopped vegetables, any combination of the following:
    onions, parsnip, cabbage, celery,
    carrot, green pepper, tomato,
    potato
Salt and pepper to taste
Pinch of marjoram
Sprinkle of dill or fennel

Combine all ingredients and simmer, covered, for several hours. Adjust seasonings, if necessary, at the end of the cooking period. We enjoy Polish sausage added to Borsht for a hearty supper dish on winter evenings. This quantity makes 6 generous servings.

SPLIT PEA SOUP

3 cups split green or yellow peas
2 quarts broth from tongue
   (or water)
  Meaty ham bone
   or 2 lbs. venison brisket
4 carrots
5 or 6 stalks of celery, leaves too

2 onions, sliced
1½ cups tomatoes
   Generous pinch thyme
2 bay leaves
   Salt and pepper to taste.

Combine ingredients and simmer in a covered kettle about 2 hours. Remove bones and meat, cut meat in small pieces and reserve. Put vegetables through a sieve or food mill, reheat with meat pieces. Garnish with croutons. If the soup is too thick for your taste, it may be thinned with milk or cream, but one of our friends maintains that 'tain't good pea soup unless you can stand the spoon up in it! If you have cooked your moose or deer tongue in camp, this is a good one to remember.

LENTIL SOUP

Lentils are an excellent trail food—easy to carry, high fuel and nutrition content, an outstanding source of protein and vitamin B. I do suggest that you soak the lentils overnight and then cook them in fresh liquid to prevent digestive upset.

1½ to 2 cups lentils, soaked
   overnight in cold water,
   drained
2 quarts of tongue or ham broth
   or 2 quarts of water plus
   diced bacon
1 onion, sliced
  Pinch of thyme or dried
   parsley

2 to 3 carrots, sliced
2 to 3 stalks celery, chopped,
   leaves too
   Salt and pepper to taste
   Bay leaf

Combine all ingredients in a covered kettle, cook slowly for 2 hours, or until lentils are tender. Press through a coarse sieve or food mill, and check seasoning. Our favorite when reheating the next day—brown sliced onions and sliced franks in butter, add soup and heat 10 minutes, until very hot. Good on a rainy day in camp—serve for lunch with dark bread and canned fruit for dessert.

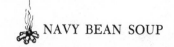 NAVY BEAN SOUP

2 cups navy beans, soaked
    at least 3 hours, drained
3 quarts venison stock
2 stalks celery, chopped
2 carrots, sliced
1 large potato, diced
1 onion, sliced
    or 1 tsp. dried onion
    Salt and pepper to taste

Pinch of thyme and marjoram
2 cups tomatoes (if available)

Cook beans in stock for 2 hours, add remainder of vegetables and cook another hour. Sieve and serve with a slice of lemon on each bowl.

***Camp suggestion for bean, pea, or lentil soup:*

If fresh vegetables are not available, use dehydrated vegetable soup, legumes, bouillon cubes and water. Set the kettle over a slow part of your dinner fire and the soup will be ready when it's time to retire. A quick reheating the next day and you have the beginning of a fine dinner.

GAME BIRD STOCK

Bones from broiled or roasted
  game birds
Veal knuckle bone, cracked
Water to cover—measure it as you add it to the kettle
1 cup of the following, chopped and blended, per quart of water:
  Carrot
  Celery and leaves
  Onion
  Salt—1 tbsp. per quart of water

Any older game bird—i.e.
  pheasant

Peppercorns—½ tsp. per quart of
  water
Parsley—several sprigs per quart
  of water

Cover the bones and bird with cold water in a large covered kettle. Bring slowly to a boil, skim and add vegetables and seasonings. Simmer covered until the bird is tender. Remove the bird from the stock, strip the meat from the bones and set aside. Return the bones to the kettle and simmer another few hours. Strain, cool, skim any fat and freeze. The meat may be used for game pies, pâtés, creamed dishes or to garnish consomme.

GAME BIRD CONSOMME

Clarify as directed earlier in the chapter. Serve as suggested previously or:
1. Garnish with diced or julienne strips of fowl plus a small can of button mushrooms
2. ½ cup finely broken noodles or ½ cup rice per quart of consomme— simmer until rice or noodles are tender—add finely chopped parsley just before serving.

GREEN PEPPER CONSOMME

I have included this recipe because it is unusual and never fails to intrigue with its delicate and delicious flavor. I like to serve it as first course with grouse or quail.

4 sweet peppers, large—may be green or tinged with red
3 medium fresh tomatoes, cut up
1 onion, sliced

6 cups water
1 tsp. salt
Pinch cloves

Remove seeds and white membrane from peppers, cut into pieces. Combine all ingredients, heat to boiling, and simmer in covered saucepan for 2 hours. Strain and adjust seasonings. This may be served hot or cold.

KARTOFFELSUPPE—*Austrian Potato Soup*

5 potatoes
2 or 3 carrots
1 celery knob or 3 stalks celery
1 medium onion, sliced
6 cups game bird stock

Salt and pepper
2 tsps. caraway seeds
2 tbsps. butter
3 tbsps. flour
Parsley, finely chopped

Peel and cube the vegetables, cover with boiling game stock, add salt and pepper, caraway seeds. Simmer covered until vegetables are tender—about 1 hour. Make a roux as follows: melt butter, stir in flour and cook over low heat until bubbly. Add 1 cup of liquid from the soup, stirring constantly until thickened and smooth. Blend into soup carefully so as not to mash vegetables and continue to cook for 5 to 10 minutes. Serve garnished with finely chopped parsley.

VICHYSSOISE

Every nation has its potato and onion soup. This is considered a French classic, although I understand it was originally created in an American hotel.

8 leeks, finely chopped
2 stalks celery, finely chopped
3 cups potatoes, finely diced
4 tbsps. butter

1 quart game bird consomme
2 cups cream
Salt and pepper

Clean leeks very thoroughly, as they are apt to be gritty. Melt the butter in a large saucepan, and cook the leeks and celery over a low flame without browning for 5 to 10 minutes Add potatoes, stock and seasonings, cover and simmer until potatoes are very tender, about 25 minutes. Put through a sieve or food mill, blend in the cream and chill. Serve in chilled bowls, garnished with chives, parsley or a dash of paprika. I usually make a double recipe of this soup and freeze only the onion and potato mixture, adding equal portions of cream to the thawed mixture when I am ready to serve it.

AVOCADO CREAM SOUP

2 cups stock from pheasant,
    grouse, or partridge
1 chicken bouillon cube
1 tbsp. cornstarch
1 cup milk
1½ tsp. grated onion

1 avocado, peeled and mashed
    with a sprinkle of lemon
    juice
Salt to taste

Bring stock to a boil, dissolve bouillon cube, slowly add cornstarch dissolved in milk. Cook over medium flame, stirring until mixture thickens—do not boil. Add onion and mashed avocado. Continue to heat for another minute or two over low flame, serve piping hot to 4 people. A garnish of crisp bacon crumbles or shredded toasted almonds is attractive.

LEMON SOUP

Speedy to prepare, light and unusually delicious for a bridge luncheon with a game bird souffle or hot pâté.

2 eggs
  Sprinkle of salt
4 tsp. cold water

3 tbsp. lemon juice
  Pinch of dried chervil, if desired
4 cups game consomme, heated

Combine all ingredients except consomme and beat well. Gradually stir in hot bouillon, place over low flame and heat only to boiling point. stirring constantly. Strain through fine sieve into preheated bouillon cups and serve immediately to 4.

MULLIGATAWNY

This dish has its origin in the East Indies and means "pepper water". It was originally made of chicken and rice, highly seasoned with curry. I have found it an excellent way to use an older pheasant or a sage hen which you might suspect to be bitter.

1 large pheasant or sage hen
4 tbsp. butter
1½ cups total of the following, chopped: onion, celery, green pepper, carrot
2 green apples, peeled and chopped
2 quarts game bird stock
1 8 oz. can tomato puree

1 tbsp. flour
1 tbsp. curry powder (start with less, if you prefer)
Pinch mace
Salt and pepper to taste

Disjoint bird, brown the pieces in a heavy kettle with the melted butter. Add the chopped vegetables and apple as the bird is browning. stirring so all browns evenly. Push the vegetables and bird to one side, add flour, curry and mace, stirring until they are well blended and bubbly. Slowly pour in the stock and tomato puree, blending until smooth. Season to taste with salt and pepper. When the broth is boiling, cover and simmer over low heat until the bird is tender. Remove the bird, dice the meat in fairly large pieces, put the vegetables through a sieve or food mill, return diced fowl and vegetable puree to broth and heat well. Serve in a tureen, with a side dish of rice. Place some rice in each bowl and ladle the soup over it.

CHESTNUT SOUP

Chestnuts have a natural affinity for game. Do try this one!

2 cups blanched chestnuts
   (see Chap. XIII for
    shelling instructions)
½ cup celery, chopped
2 tbsps. finely minced onion
¼ cup butter
3 tbsps. flour

1 tsp. salt
¼ tsp. pepper
Blade of mace
2 whole cloves
2 cups game stock
1 cup cream

Cook chestnuts and celery in lightly salted water 15 to 20 minutes, drain and force through food mill. Set puree aside. In large saucepan, melt butter and cook onion over low heat without browning for 5 minutes. Blend in flour until smooth and bubbly, add salt, pepper, mace and cloves. Pour in stock slowly, stirring constantly until it thickens. Remove mace and cloves. Combine cream and chestnut puree and blend into stock. Reheat until piping hot, but do not boil.

CREAM SOUPS

There are countless varieties of creamed soups—the choice is limited only by your own imagination. This is a basic recipe I have worked out, with a few suggestions for vegetable combinations. The rest is up to you.

4 tbsps. roux (see Chap. X)
  Salt and pepper to taste
2 cups total of the following:
  Game bird stock (or chicken
    broth)

Liquid in which the vegetables
  were cooked
2 cups light cream
2 cups vegetable puree

Cook vegetables in lightly salted water to cover—don't drown the vegetables! Drain and reserve the liquid. Combine vegetable liquid with enough game bird stock to make 2 cups. Puree vegetables. Melt roux in saucepan and stir over low heat until bubbly, add seasonings. Slowly stir in vegetable and game stock, blending until smooth and thickened. Add cream and vegetable puree, continue to cook over low flame until very hot, but do not allow to boil once cream has been added. A bit of grated onion or a sprinkle of freshly grated nutmeg may add needed zest.

Suggested vegetable combinations:

Mushroom and celery

Spinach and watercress (cook over low heat with only the water which
   clings to the leaves
Asparagus and celery (reserve the asparagus tips for garnish)
Carrot and onion
Cabbage and onion (garnish with grated sharp cheddar cheese)
Cooked cucumber and celery, with 1 tbsp. each chopped green pepper
   and onion
   Any leftover soup will be a welcome addition to a casserole. When
I freeze these soups, I combine only the vegetable puree with the stock,
preferring to add the cream in proper proportion after the stock has
been reheated.

   Since most hunters enjoy fishing as well, I have included two fish
recipes that are particularly suited to camp cooking.

FISH MULLIGAN

I have often wondered if the name "mulligan" has any relation to the
East Indian mulligatawny—at any rate, it's a good camp dish—add,
subtract or substitute whatever is handy.

2 lbs. fish, cut in chunks	1 green pepper, diced
4 potatoes, diced	2 or 3 strips bacon, diced
2 onions, sliced	Celery or celery salt
1½ quarts water	Carrots or any leftover
⅓ cup raw rice	vegetables

   In a large kettle combine fish, potatoes, onions and water. Bring to
a vigorous boil, then add rice, green pepper and bacon, plus any other
vegetables you may have on hand. Cover and remove to a spot on the
cooking fire where it will just simmer until the potatoes are done—
about ½ hour.

FISH CHOWDER

3 or 4 strips bacon, diced	2 cups milk
1 large onion, sliced	(canned milk or equivalent
2 lbs. fish, cut in pieces	dried milk and water)
6 potatoes, sliced	1 tsp. salt
Water to cover	Pepper to taste

1 tbsp. butter   Parsley, fresh or dried
1 tbsp. flour

Brown bacon in kettle, remove browned bits and set aside. In the bacon fat, cook sliced onion until golden brown. Add fish and potatoes, barely cover with water. Set beside the fire to simmer gently until the potatoes are tender. Blend butter and flour, thin with a small amount of the pot liquid, add to fish and potatoes and stir until thickened. Add milk and seasonings to taste, simmer 5 more minutes. A can of corn, drained, is also a nice addition to this chowder.

RABBIT SOUP

If the rabbit population is over-abundant, you might try this soup as a change from stew, roast or fried rabbit. It's particularly suited to older critters.

1 old rabbit or hare   1 tsp. grated lemon peel
2 cups chopped soup vegetables,   ¼ cup butter (or
  including the following: more, if necessary)
    carrot, onion, celery knob,   2 quarts stock
    turnip (or parsnip)   Salt and pepper to taste
2 or 3 sprigs parsley   1 tbsp. roux
1 bay leaf   1 wine glass port or sauterne
  Pinch rosemary

Brown disjointed rabbit with vegetables and herbs in melted butter. Add stock and lemon peel and simmer on low flame for several hours—until rabbit is very tender. Season to taste with salt and pepper. Strain soup through colander, remove rabbit meat from bones and cut into cubes. Puree vegetables, and return puree to broth along with diced meat. Thicken with roux, stir until smooth, add wine and serve.

CHAPTER III

Big Game

CONTRARY TO POPULAR BELIEF, cooking of game (especially the larger animals) requires no magic incantations or involved recipes. With the meat properly cared for from the time the game was shot, no unpleasant taste needs to be overcome by marinating in a witch's potion, nor does the flavor need to be masked by a great assortment of herbs and spices. The flavor of game is delicious as is—and the simpler the recipe, the better, in most cases.

When people have commented favorably on game served in our home and then said, "But it must be so complicated to cook it right", my answer has always been, "No, it's really quite simple." I have not been trying to sound modest, and I shall probably ruin my reputation as a game cook by stating flatly that it *is* simple. The weird contortions so often recommended are those needed to disguise the flavor of spoiled meat. If you've been with me thus far, you can serve a dinner to please even the most discriminating gourmet without spending hours in the kitchen. The major battle was won before the game ever reached the kitchen—and that's as it should be.

There are a few basic principles involved—and that's all! First, and most important: the animal fat which has already been removed must be replaced in some fashion to prevent dryness. This is done by larding (drawing strips of fat pork through the meat with a larding needle), by wrapping the meat in bacon, by using beef suet or butter.

Second: treat each animal individually. Game is not standardized as beef is. It only stands to reason that a large bull elk or moose will require a slightly different approach in the kitchen than an antelope doe or a young deer. When I was learning to cook, I was always dreadfully annoyed when Mother said, "Just cook it until it's done"—it seemed to me then a most unscientific attitude! Now I can appreciate her wisdom, for the cooking time "until done"—and even the cooking method—will vary greatly from one animal to the next, even in the same species. So throw away the rule books and the timers and let your intuition take over.

Basically, antelope, caribou, deer, elk, moose and reindeer are all cooked in the same manner as beef. *Antelope* is a most delicate and deliciously flavored meat, which requires little adornment. *Caribou,* with its diet of moss and lichens, is juicy and flavorful. *Deer,* including the mule, blacktail and whitetail, is the most widely known to the great majority of hunters and certainly ranks high on the scale of good eating. *Elk* is considered by some to be the very best of all and they compare it to prime beef. *Moose,* the largest member of the deer family, is considered most desirable for the table when shot in late August or early September. During the rut, from the middle of September to November, the meat of the bull is apt to be stringy and to have a very strong flavor. *Reindeer,* practically a staple in the diet of Alaskans, has not quite as delicate a flavor as deer.

Bear should be cooked in the same manner as pork—that is, *always* well done—because of the possibility of trichinosis. The excess fat is always trimmed off and may be rendered for use as shortening. I've never used it myself, but those who have prefer it to all others. *Wild boar,* or the wild hog which is a cross between the Russian boar and the razorback, is also cooked like domestic pork. The young ones are particularly good, but even the old tuskers are delicious after some tenderizing. After all, long slow cooking is necessary for porkers anyway.

Since our remaining bison herds are protected, most of us will have little chance of cooking *buffalo* meat. However, if you are fortunate enough to participate in the occasional hunt to reduce a herd to proper size for its range, cook the meat as you would for any pot roast, removing the fat first.

Goats are hunted primarily for their trophy heads and the flesh of the billies is considered by many to be tough and strong, although still edible before the rut. The flesh of the nannies is excellent. The *sheep* are prized not only for their trophy heads, but for their meat. Wild mutton ranks high in the gourmet class. As with domestic mutton, the fat is unappetizing and should be removed before cooking.

The basic rule for cooking game is the same as for any meat: roast or broil the tender cuts, braise or stew the tougher ones. The tender cuts are, of course, the saddle and the haunch; the tougher ones the forequarter and the shank. However, what is tender enough for roasting or broiling on a young animal may require a period of long slow cooking on a really mature beast. Round steak, from the top of the hind leg, is a perfect example. I have had marvelously tender steaks from antelope and 3 year old deer, broiled over charcoal until they were just pink inside. The same broiling method was *not* successful with the same cut from a patriarch of an Idaho elk herd. It would have been, however, had the round steaks been from a cow or yearling elk.

But how do you decide on the appropriate method for all that meat in the freezer? One test made on a round steak in the privacy of your own family will give you a very good indication of how you should proceed the rest of the winter.

Occasionally it happens to all of us that we are given a piece of game, with no indication of its age or tenderness. When in doubt, use any one of the non-seasoned meat tenderizers as directed on the package or use the long slow method.

So far I have not mentioned marinating as a means of tenderizing. Some game cooks will recommend it to you for practically everything— not I! I concede that the acid in a marinade (usually wine vinegar) will help somewhat in tenderizing, but I have also noticed that most of these same recipes still require long slow cooking. Many claim that it eliminates the strong gamey flavor, others state equally as vehemently that it enhances the gamey flavor. You pays your money and you takes your choice! As for me, I'll skip the marinade nine times out of ten and stick to the long slow cooking method with a mildly acid ingredient such as lemon, tomato or dry wine, cooked with the meat. These complement and enhance the flavor of the meat, but don't dominate it as a marinade does so frequently. The one exception I make in favor of a marinade is in preparation of some of the classic German and Austrian dishes—there the sweet-sour tang is expected and appropriate. This is only one person's opinion, however, so try it both ways and make your own decision.

ROASTS AND CHOPS

Every cook has a favorite way of cooking a roast of beef. There are so many new gadgets on the market, including electric spits, meat thermometers that serenade you and ovens that do everything but darn your socks, that there is no longer any hard and fast rule for turning out an excellent roast. Follow any method you prefer, as long as the result is a roast attractively browned on the outside, yet still rare and tender in the middle, with a rich brown gravy. If your family is adamant in their preference for well-done roasts, then you'd better stick to the pot roast versions, since venison roasts are tender and juicy when done only to the medium-rare stage.

With backyard cooking as well as camp cooking becoming more and more popular, many men have turned into excellent chefs, especially when it comes to steaks and chops. Again, use any of the means of broiling that you think produces the best steaks. One of our friends tells of a venerable and highly esteemed camp cook who set a huge kettle of deep fat on the fire until it was bubbling and sputtering. He then drew each steak slowly through the boiling fat with tongs. Our friend admits that he was horrified as he witnessed the whole operation, but delightfully surprised when he tasted the delectable results. I don't necessarily advocate your trying this method—I only mention it to prove that there are many means to the same end.

There is only one problem in broiling game steaks and chops. Somehow you must add fat to the meat so it doesn't dry out. Remember there is no thick rim of fat on a properly prepared venison steak. *Do* salt your steak *after* broiling and use only freshly ground pepper, even if you've never bothered with it before. You're preparing one of the most delectable meats possible and it deserves only the finest ingredients! Six to eight minutes for a 1″ thick steak, a sizzling platter and a lump of fresh butter—that's it! Forget the A-1 sauce, my friend—you won't want it!

ROAST VENISON

Suitable for any tender leg, loin or rib roast of the antlered game.

Preheat oven to 450°. Insert long thin strips of salt pork into the roast with a larding needle or tie bacon strips over the roast. Sprinkle flour lightly into the bottom of the roasting pan, place the roast on the flour, season with freshly ground pepper and strew a few rosemary leaves in the pan. Brown at 450° for 15 minutes, add 1 cup game stock and roast 12 to 15 minutes per pound at 325°, basting several times with the pan juices. If the roast is rather small in diameter, reduce the roasting time 2 or 3 minutes per pound.

Gravy may be made in the usual manner, substituting game stock for water, or the pan juices may be combined with 1 cup Cumberland sauce (see Chap. X) and heated just to the boiling point. Wild rice or chestnut puree would be good companions.

RUMP ROAST—*Elk or Venison*

We've heard it over and over—red meat, red wine—but do try this one! Some rules are made to be broken.

Place a rump roast in a deep glass or earthen-ware dish, cover with dry white wine and bring to room temperature (1½ to 2 hours). Remove the roast and reserve the wine. Lard roast with salt pork, season with salt and ground pepper. Roast in preheated oven at 450° 15 to 20 minutes, reduce heat to 300° to 325°, and roast 15 minutes per pound covered, basting frequently with the reserved white wine. Serve with Russian game sauce. (see Chap. X)

MOOSE OR REINDEER LEG ROAST

6 lb. roast from hind leg
  (haunch)
¼ cup butter
4 or 5 sprigs parsley, minced
½ tsp. dried savory, crumbled
½ tsp. dried tarragon, crumbled

10 to 12 juniper berries, crushed
1 cup red wine or equal parts
  wine and game stock
Salt and pepper

Melt butter without browning, add herbs and cook together several minutes. Place roast, seasoned with salt and pepper and lightly sprinkled with flour, in roasting pan. Pour over savory butter and place in oven which has been preheated to 450°. After 20 minutes, reduce heat to 325°, add wine and stock, cover and roast 25 minutes per pound, basting frequently. When roast is tender, remove to a heated platter and keep warm while you prepare the sauce.

Add 1 cup game stock to the juices in the roasting pan, set over flame and stir briskly to loosen any crusty bits in the pan. Strain through a sieve into a small saucepan, add ¼ cup currant jelly, ½ cup red wine, 1 tbsp. brandy, 1½ tbsp. roux. Stir briskly until sauce is smooth and thickened. Allow to simmer a few minutes and pour into preheated serving boat.

(If juniper berries are difficult to find in your area, write to one of the companies specializing in herbs and spices. In the meantime until your juniper berries arrive, substitute equal parts of gin and stock for the red wine and achieve practically the same results, since the main flavoring ingredient in gin is the juniper berry.)

BEAR RUMP ROAST

Suitable for a young animal. Saddle or leg could also be used.

Cut 1 clove of garlic into small slivers, insert in gashes in the roast, season with salt and freshly ground pepper. Lard or tie with bacon or fat pork (adjust salt if you are using bacon). Roast uncovered at 325° for 35 to 45 minutes per pound, with just enough beef bouillon or red wine to cover the bottom of the roasting pan. Baste frequently with the pan juices, adding more liquid if necessary. Make gravy of the pan juices, serve with noodles and currant or wild blueberry jelly. Or make the gravy with the currant jelly added to it.

BARBECUED BEAR LEG

This is where the men take over! Spit the bear leg and roast over deep bed of coals in a pit. Be sure you're on sandy or clay soil, not humus or root-filled soil, especially where shallow-rooted evergreens are present. The fire in your cooking pit could start such roots smoldering and the results are disastrous. To get back to your bear—baste frequently with your favorite barbecue sauce, made in rather large quantities, for this will be a fairly lengthy procedure. Remember that bear must be well done—the time, of course, will depend not only of the bear's size, but upon your fire. (If you'd care to try another sauce from the one you usually use, there are several listed in Chap. X.)

ROAST SADDLE OF BEAR

Combine the following:

1 cup cider	1 tbsp. lemon juice
2 tbsp. soy sauce	2 tbsp. honey
1 tsp. ginger	

Season with salt and pepper and then lard a saddle of bear. Pour over the combined liquids and roast as directed for bear rump roast, basting with the pan juices. This is also excellent served cold with any of the game sauces in Chap. X.

SADDLE OF BOAR

Season the saddle of a young boar with salt and freshly ground black pepper, sprinkle on some poultry seasoning (the type you normally use for turkey stuffing) or crumble a few dried savory leaves in the bottom of the roasting pan. Roast uncovered in a slow oven 325° for 35 minutes per pound, basting with the pan drippings. If desired, a small amount of water may be placed in the bottom of the pan. Make gravy with the pan juices and serve with sweet potatoes and gooseberry sauce. (see Chaps. IX and XIII)

BONED BOAR HAM EPICURE

*Stuffed with prune and apple stuffing,
a boar leg served in this manner is not
only attractive, but tastes as good as
it looks. This presentation of a boned
ham is festive, yet really simple to
prepare. The most important ingredient
is a razor-sharp boning knife and, of
course, the desire to serve a delicious
meal in an appealing way.*

BONED BOAR HAM EPICURE

With thin, sharp boning knife, remove the bone from the whole ham, working from the underside where the bone is closest to the surface. Stuff the pocket lightly with prune and apple stuffing or sage and onion stuffing (see Chap. X)—be sure to allow for expansion of the stuffing. With a curved needle, such as is used for upholstery work, sew up the opening, catching sufficient flesh in the sewing process so that the stitching won't pull out as the ham is cooked. Season ham with salt and pepper (plus poultry seasoning if sage dressing was used), and roast at 350° for 30 minutes per pound, basting with pan drippings. Any additional stuffing may be baked in the roasting pan, or in a separate tin, the last hour. Make gravy in the usual fashion. Garnish the platter with glazed apple slices, glazed oranges or rosy spiced crab apples. (Remove all evidence of your surgery—the string—before serving, of course.) Your husband will be delighted not to have to carve around the bone, and I believe your guests will be impressed with the stuffing-centered slices.

ROAST CARIBOU

Lard with salt pork a saddle or rump roast of young caribou. Either insert slivers of garlic into gashes in the roast or arrange slices of onion in the bottom of the roasting pan. Season with salt and pepper, add a bay leaf and 2 chopped stalks of celery, including the tops, to the roaster. Sear at 450° 15 to 20 minutes, then roast covered at 300° for 15 minutes per pound, basting every 20 minutes with cider or red wine. Remove roast to a heated platter, keep warm while you make the gravy. Skim off any excess fat, heat pan juices to boiling point, scraping sides of roaster to loosen any browned particles, adding a bit more wine or cider if necessary. Strain into small saucepan, then slowly add 1 cup sour cream, stirring constantly. Heat just to boiling point, but do not allow gravy to boil once sour cream has been added.

CROWN ROAST OF VENISON

This is truly a noble feast—well worth the use of all the rib chops at once. Your butcher will probably have a hand in the preparation of the roast, but you will still be paying your mighty hunter a fine compliment when you match his skill in the field with yours in the kitchen.

The preparation of a crown roast is really quite simple, but does require a skilled hand with the saw and butcher knife. The backbone is removed from sufficient of the rib chops to make an attractive crown, usually a part, if not all, of the two racks. The rib bones are left rather long so they curve outwardly as the meat section is turned to the center. The whole is firmly tied or sewed together. Have the butcher trim all fat and return the meat trimmings as well as the backbone to you.

Simmer the bones and meat trimmings as directed in Chap. II for stock needed in the balance of the recipe.

6 to 7 cups game stock or beef bouillon for gravy and stuffing
2 cups each finely chopped onions and celery
¼ cup butter
½ lb. ground venison or mildly seasoned sausage

2 cups long grain rice (not the precooked kind!)
Salt and freshly ground pepper to taste
½ tsp. thyme
½ tsp. marjoram
1 tbsp. parsley, finely chopped
3 eggs, slightly beaten

In a large skillet, sauté onion, celery, and meat in butter until all is lightly browned, stirring to blend. Add rice, seasonings and two cups of stock, mixing well. Cover and simmer over low flame until the liquid has been absorbed by the rice, stirring occasionally so it doesn't stick to the pan. Check seasonings and allow stuffing to cool. Add slightly beaten eggs and mix thoroughly. Brush roast liberally with butter. Preheat oven to 450°, place roast on rack in the roasting pan, covering the rib ends with foil to prevent charring, and sear for 15 minutes. Place 1 cup water or stock in the bottom of the roaster, fill center of the roast with stuffing, mounding it attractively, and return to 350° oven. Roast 12 to 15 minutes per pound or better yet, use a meat thermometer inserted carefully between the ribs and roast only to the medium rare stage. Baste the outside of the ribs once in a while and cover the top of the stuffing with foil if it begins to get too brown.

When the roast is done, transfer to your most elegant platter, remove the strings and foil and keep warm while you prepare the gravy. Add 3 cups stock to the roaster, set over the flame and bring to a boil. Stir to loosen any browned residue in the pan, and thicken with a flour and water paste. Check seasoning of the gravy and allow to simmer 5 minutes. Garnish rib ends with crab apples and decorate the platter with additional apples and sprigs of parsley. Keep the vegetables simple, but elegant. (See Chap. XIII for suggestions) To carve, just slice down between the ribs.

FRUIT GLAZED VENISON ROAST

This is a pleasant variation in flavor, suitable for all the antlered game.

Lard roast with salt pork, season with salt and pepper, and sear at 450° for 15 minutes. Reduce oven heat to 325° and cook covered for 12 minutes per pound, basting frequently with a blend of the following ingredients:

1 cup orange juice
  Generous pinch allspice
  1 tbsp. lemon juice

20 minutes before the roast is done, brush with the following glaze:

2 tbsp. butter
2 tbsp. orange juice
  ½ cup tart jelly—
      crab apple or currant

Serve with glazed orange slices, wild rice and mushrooms.

MOUNTAIN SHEEP ROAST

Roast from hind leg or saddle   Salt and pepper
Lemon juice   Garlic, if desired, or rosemary
Cooking oil

Remove all fat possible, rub the roast with lemon juice and then brush with cooking oil. Season with salt and freshly ground pepper, insert slivers of garlic in the roast or sprinkle a few rosemary leaves in the bottom of the roaster. Sear in preheated oven at 475° until browned, about 20 minutes. Add water to cover bottom of pan and roast at 300° 25 minutes per pound until tender, basting frequently. Mint jelly, parsley buttered new potatoes and fresh peas are traditional, but you might also try curried rice, for a change of pace. (see Chap. XIII)

ROAST SADDLE OF GOAT

In glass or earthen-ware bowl, marinate the roast for two days in the following blend:

1 cup white wine or
½ cup water
½ cup wine or cider vinegar
1 tsp. salt

1 thinly sliced onion
8 or 10 crushed peppercorns
2 bay leaves
4 tbsp. salad oil

Cover and set in a cool place, turning the meat at least once or twice a day. Remove from marinade, drain and pat dry. Sprinkle lightly with flour, salt and ground pepper, and crumbled savory leaves. Preheat oven to 475°, roast for 15 to 20 minutes, then lower oven temperature to 325° and roast ½ hour per pound, basting frequently with a blend of ¼ cup melted butter, ½ cup water and 2 tsp. lemon juice.

I have only one or two suggestions on the subject of steaks and chops. If you have decided to have the backstrap removed in one piece and frozen solid, as I have mentioned before, then cut your filets across the grain about twice as thick as you like your steak to be (2″). Place each filet between 2 sheets of waxed paper and whack it with the flat side of your cleaver. This will help to tenderize the meat and will also provide a good sized filet of the proper thickness (1″).

Dip chops or steaks in melted butter or the finest olive oil before broiling. Bone chops and wrap each in a strip of bacon, skewering it neatly in place. Season after broiling.

A nice addition, but not really necessary, is the use of seasoned butters, added after the steaks are on the platter. (see Chap. X)

Have your guests assembled, the rest of the dinner completed and ready to put on the table, the steak platter sizzling hot—then broil your steaks! 6 to 8 minutes total time for a 1″ steak is about the maximum!

POT ROASTS AND STEWS

No one need ever hesitate about serving a game pot roast or stew to guests. Well cooked and attractively served, these are the perfect winter meals. The hostess, too, has the advantage of very little fuss in the kitchen at the last minute, since these dishes tend to themselves very nicely over a low flame.

SAUERBRATEN

Moose, elk, deer, caribou, or reindeer may be used for this recipe.

4 lb. rump or blade pot roast

2 slices bacon, cubed

Marinade:
Boil together 5 minutes and
cool the following:
3 cups water
1½ cups vinegar
2 bay leaves

12 whole peppercorns
2 or 3 cloves
1 sliced carrot
1 sliced onion
2 stalks celery, sliced

Gravy:
12 gingersnaps
4 tbsps. roux
3 to 4 tbsps. sour cream

Place meat in a glass or pottery bowl—never metal! Pour over the cooled marinade—liquid must cover the meat. Keep in a cool place 3 to 4 days, turning meat once a day.

In dutch oven, brown diced bacon and then remove the crisp bits and set aside. Drain the meat, pat dry, brown in hot bacon fat and then season with salt. Add half the marinade as well as the vegetables from the marinade and the crisp bacon and bring the liquid to a boil. Reduce the flame to the lowest possible point and simmer, covered, until tender, adding more marinade if necessary. Turn occasionally with spoon and tongs—don't pierce the meat! The cooking time will depend on the age and tenderness of the meat—at least 2½ to 3 hours. When fork tender, remove to hot platter and keep warm.

Bring marinade (including reserved) to a boil, add broken gingersnaps and roux, stirring together until thickened. Strain through a sieve, add sour cream and reheat over a low flame for 3 to 4 minutes —do not boil! Serve with Kartoffelknödel (potato dumplings) and red cabbage. (see Chaps. XII and XIII)

POT ROAST OF BIG GAME (*including bear*)

Shoulder or rump roast
Flour
Salt and pepper
Bacon drippings
2 sliced carrots
2 stalks celery chopped,
   including the leaves

2 sliced onions
2 cups canned tomatoes
2 bay leaves
½ tsp. ground cloves
½ tsp. thyme
¼ tsp. allspice

Coat the meat on all sides with seasoned flour, brown in dutch oven in hot fat, turning to brown all sides. Add carrots, celery and onions during the last of the browning process. Add tomatoes and spices, cover and simmer *very* slowly, with the liquid barely bubbling, until tender, at *least* 4 hours. After 2 hours of cooking, turn the meat over in the pot and thereafter, check occasionally to be sure there is enough liquid in the pot. Remove the meat to a hot platter, discard bay leaves, and put sauce through food mill or sieve. Return sauce to the pot and reheat to the boiling point. Serve with broad buttered noodles. Baked carrots and onions are a very good vegetable accompaniment.

VENISON À LA MODE

This is an adaptation of the French classic, Boeuf à la Mode, which means "in the current fashion", and not with ice cream on top!

4 lbs. boneless rump, round,   1 bunch carrots, quartered
   or chuck roast   1 doz. small white onions
Salt pork
¼ cup drippings
1 clove garlic
2 or 3 shallots or ¼ cup
   chopped onion
Bouquet garni (parsley, thyme,
   bay leaf tied together)
1 cup white wine
¼ cup brandy
1 veal knuckle bone

Cut larding pork in long thin strips and marinate in brandy for one hour. Lard the roast, reserving the brandy. In a dutch oven, brown the meat in drippings, turning so all sides are browned. Season with salt and freshly ground pepper. Add all remaining ingredients except carrots and onions, including brandy. Cover and simmer over very low flame until almost completely tender—at least 4 hours. Add carrots and whole onions, continue to simmer until vegetables are tender— about 45 minutes. Remove bouquet garni and knuckle bone, check seasoning and thicken gravy. Serve roast with vegetables arranged around it. Pour some gravy over the roast, serve remainder in a sauce boat. Crusty French bread, (see Chap. XII) a crisp salad, fruit and cheese for dessert.

"DOWN EAST" POT ROAST

4 lbs. boneless rump, round,
    or chuck roast
    Drippings
    Salt and pepper, flour
2 cups cranberries
1 cup water
    Sprinkle of allspice
4 whole cloves

    Orange juice
2 tbsp. sugar
½ cup tart jelly

Coat meat with flour, seasoned with salt and pepper, brown in hot drippings in dutch oven. In the meantime, cook cranberries in water until skins pop, then pour over browned meat. Add allspice and cloves. Cover and simmer on low flame. As meat cooks, maintain level of liquid with orange juice rather than water. When meat is tender, remove meat to hot platter, strain pot liquid into small saucepan, add sugar and tart jelly. Heat thoroughly and thicken if necessary with flour and water paste. Instead of the usual noodles, you might try skillet corn bread or New England Jonny cake with this one. (see Chap. XII)

BOAR—*Austrian Style*

This is not in the actual pot roast category, but this is the most appropriate place for dealing with that aged tusker.

    Boar shoulder joint
    Salted water to cover
1 cup vinegar
2 cups water
2 cups red wine
2 sliced onions
    Soup greens: carrot, celery,
        parsnip, parsley

1 bay leaf
10 to 12 whole peppercorns
10 to 12 juniper berries

Simmer shoulder joint in salted water to cover for 1½ hours. Drain and return to kettle with the remaining ingredients. Cover and simmer until tender. Slice meat and arrange on hot platter, keep warm. Make gravy from 2 cups of the cooking liquid, enough roux to thicken, then add 1 cup cranberry sauce.

SHEEP—*English Style*

Leg of sheep	½ lemon, sliced thin
1 bay leaf	1 tsp. salt
1 sliced onion	Water to cover

To eliminate the possibility of strong flavor, remove all fat from leg. In large kettle, cover joint with boiling water, and boil hard for 10 minutes. Skim any fat that rises, add bay leaf, onion and lemon and simmer, covered until tender. Add salt halfway through cooking period. Serve with caper sauce. (see Chap. X)

SHEEP OR GOAT—*Scandinavian Style With Dill*

The basic method is the same as the English recipe—the difference is in the seasoning. If you have only a tiny plot of land, by all means plant some dill next year—it has dozens of uses in the kitchen—in breads, fish dishes, vegetables and salads, as well as dill pickles. The feathery leaves can be frozen in small packages for year 'round use.

Shoulder or leg roast	2 tbsp. lemon juice or vinegar
Water to cover	2 tsp. sugar
1 tbsp. salt for each	3 tbsp. finely snipped dill
2 quarts of water	
6 sprigs fresh dill or a generous	
pinch of dill seed	
1 cup medium white sauce	

Put meat in large kettle, add water to cover, measuring as you do so. Add proportionate amount of salt and dill. Bring to a boil uncovered, skim foam. Cover and simmer slowly until tender. Remove to a warm serving platter and keep warm until the meat has a chance to firm up (about 20 minutes). Prepare white sauce, add vinegar or lemon juice, sugar and snipped dill. Carve the meat in thin slices, arrange on platter, pour over some of the sauce and serve the rest in a sauce boat. Red cabbage or beets would be good here.

POT ROAST WITH SOUR CREAM SAUCE

Suitable for buffalo as well as antlered game.

Rump or shoulder roast	Pinch thyme
Drippings	Few juniper berries
Salt and pepper	1 lemon, sliced thin
1 onion, sliced	1 cup red wine
2 carrots, sliced	1 cup game stock
1 small turnip, diced	½ cup sour cream
2 stalks celery, sliced	1 bay leaf

In dutch oven, brown seasoned meat and vegetables together in hot drippings. Add herbs, lemon, wine and game stock. Cover and simmer over very low flame for 2 hours. Remove meat, strain sauce back into pot, pressing vegetables through the sieve. Add sour cream to the sauce, and blend, return meat to the pot and simmer very gently until tender. Serve with rice, cranberries and green vegetable.

STUFFED SHOULDER OF VENISON

Stuff boned shoulder roast with any savory stuffing of your choice, being sure that the stuffing is not too moist—the steam generated in the braising process will make it soggy if it's moist to begin with. Tie or sew the roast together, sear on all sides in heavy skillet in hot fat, adding carrot and onion slices if you wish. Season with salt and pepper and add enough game stock to fill skillet ½" deep. Cover and simmer on low flame until tender, adding more stock if needed. Remove roast to serving platter, remove string and thicken gravy if necessary.

HUNGARIAN GOULASH

Hungarians usually make their national stew with veal—occasionally with beef. However, any stew meat of the deer family is an excellent substitute. This is my Mother-in-law's recipe, one I have enjoyed many times.

3 lbs. stew meat	Butter
1½ lbs. onions, sliced thin	Paprika
2 or 3 green peppers,	Salt and pepper
cut in 1" pieces	½ cup sour cream

Melt butter in heavy covered saucepan, put in thinly sliced onions and simmer until they are golden in color. Add 2 tsps. paprika (more if you are not using the real Hungarian paprika), add 1 soup ladle of water, cook until the water evaporates, repeat with the soup ladle of water, add meat, green pepper and salt and pepper. Barely cover with water and simmer on very low flame covered until the meat is tender, adding more water if necessary. Thicken gravy with 1 tbsp. roux, stir well, add sour cream and heat just below boiling point, stirring constantly. Serve with rice, noodles or dumplings.

Stew is just stew, you say disdainfully? Well, perhaps we're just peasants at heart, but in our opinion, a properly prepared stew—with succulent pieces of meat and vegetables still crisply tender, all in a rich and savory sauce—is a meal fit for a king! Biscuits baked separately to soak up that delicious gravy, or dumplings added to the pot the last few minutes—you can't ask for anything better.

Stews are ideal for camp cooking—the browned meat can be left to simmer in the dutch oven all day (either in a pit of coals or over a carefully banked fire). When you return to camp, dinner is ready in a jiffy—add vegetables to the pot and while they are simmering, whip up a batch of biscuits or dumplings, make coffee—and dig in!

At home, I usually prepare a double amount of meat and sauce. When the meat is tender, I remove half the meat and sauce, cool and freeze it in quart containers. Then I have only to add fresh vegetables for a delectable meal on short notice. Vegetables, completely cooked in a stew and then frozen, tend to become mushy when reheated— one of my pet peeves!

 VENISON STEW

All of the seasonings listed may not be available in camp, but proceed without them—hunger is still the best seasoning.

3 lbs. game, cut into 2″ cubes	Salt and pepper
¼ cup drippings	Dash of paprika
Boiling water or stock to cover	Pinch cloves or allspice
Juice of ½ lemon	Carrots, small whole or
Dash of Worcestershire sauce	quartered lengthwise
1 clove of garlic	Small white onions (cut an X
2 onions, sliced	in top and bottom so they
2 or 3 bay leaves	won't separate in cooking)
	Potatoes, cut in cubes

Brown the meat thoroughly in hot fat in the dutch oven—don't use

VENISON STEW

You'll have to call only once when this hearty country supper is ready for the table, especially when there's a wintry nip in the air. Since the stew will take care of itself on a very low flame all day, why not add the aroma of freshly baked herb biscuits or whole wheat bread to the savory odors wafting from the stew kettle?

all the drippings at once, but add as necessary. I prefer to brown only a part of the meat at a time, then remove it to a plate—this way you can be certain all is browned evenly. Return all the meat to the pot, add water or stock and seasonings, including garlic and sliced onions. Cover and simmer over very low flame until the meat is almost completely tender, stirring occasionally to prevent sticking and adding a bit more liquid if necessary. Add vegetables and continue to simmer 20 to 30 minutes—only until the vegetables are tender—don't let them disintegrate! Check for the need of additional salt during the last 15 minutes—the addition of the vegetables may require it. If you haven't drowned the meat in liquid, the gravy should not need thickening, but if it does, blend flour and water to a smooth paste and add drop by drop, stirring carefully so as not to break the vegetables.

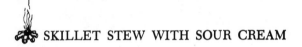

SKILLET STEW WITH SOUR CREAM

3 lbs. stew meat, cubed	2 cups evaporated milk, plus
Drippings	2½ tbsps. vinegar
1 onion, sliced	or lemon juice
Salt and pepper	Generous dash of paprika
3 cups canned tomatoes	
2 cups sour cream or	

In a heavy iron skillet, brown meat and onions in drippings. Season with salt and pepper, add tomatoes and sour cream along with paprika. Cover the skillet and set over lowest possible fire, so the liquid is barely bubbling. Stir once in a while and restrain yourself until the meat is really tender—about 2 or 3 hours. Plain boiled potatoes, noodles or rice are served with it.

IRISH STEW

Excellent for that goat or sheep.

3 lbs. neck or shoulder meat, cubed and trimmed of all fat	Water to cover
Drippings	Small whole onions
Salt and pepper	Carrots
Bouquet garni (parsley, thyme and bay leaf tied together)	Turnip, diced (if available)
	Potatoes

Brown the meat in drippings, season with salt and pepper, add water to cover and herbs. Cover and simmer on low heat until tender. Add turnip, carrots, onions and potatoes and cook for about ½ hour longer. Herb biscuits or parsley dumplings are a tasty accompaniment. (see Chap. XII)

VENISON STEW—*French Style*

Unless yours is a deluxe camp, this adaptation of Boeuf à la Bourguignonne had best be made at home.

3 lbs. stew meat, cubed	Parsley, thyme, bay leaf and a
Drippings	few celery leaves tied together
Salt and pepper	1 cup Burgundy wine
1 large onion, minced	Mushrooms, sautéed in butter
1 cup stock	Small whole onions,
3 tbsps. roux	parboiled for 6 to 8 minutes.
4 tbsps. tomato paste	

Brown meat in drippings, season with salt and pepper, and remove from skillet. Add minced onion to skillet and cook briefly—do not brown. Add stock, roux and tomato paste to onion and stir constantly as you bring the mixture to a boil. When all is smooth, replace meat, add Burgundy and herb bouquet. Cover and simmer over low heat until meat is tender. 15 minutes before serving, add mushrooms and onions to contents of skillet and continue to simmer until the flavors are blended. Serve with noodles or macaroni.

ROUND STEAK AND VARIATIONS

As I have mentioned before, the steaks from the hind leg of a mature animal will frequently require long slow cooking to.be tender. Swiss steak always comes to mind in this instance, but one can tire of it. The variations I have included here will, I hope, encourage you to go even farther afield and develop your own variations.

SWISS STEAK — *For Buffalo or Antlered Big Game*

Round steak, at least 1″ thick	Chopped onion
Flour	Bay leaf

Salt and pepper   Canned tomatoes or V-8 juice

Combine flour, salt and pepper and pound into steak with the back of the cleaver or the edge of a plate. In heavy skillet, brown on both sides in drippings, along with onion. Add tomatoes or V-8, bay leaf. Cover and simmer until tender. I have, on occasion, substituted chili sauce for the onion and tomato, with equally successful results. Our old family recipe for Chili Sauce is included in Chap. X.

STUFFED VENISON FLANK STEAK (*or round steak*)

For flank steak, score in criss-cross fashion diagonally against the grain of the meat on both sides. For round steak, pound lightly with edge of plate. Spread with any favorite stuffing (mushroom and rice, sage and onion bread stuffing). Roll and tie or skewer firmly. Brown in hot drippings or butter on all sides. Season with salt and pepper. Decrease heat to lowest possible point, add enough game stock or beef bouillon to barely cover the bottom of the skillet. Cover and simmer slowly until fork tender, adding more stock if necessary. The gravy may be thickened with a cornstarch and water paste.

VENISON—SAUTE CHASSEUR (*Hunter's Style*)

2 lbs. round steak,   1 cup dry white wine
   cut in serving portions   1 cup bouillon or stock
¼ cup butter   Bouquet garni
½ lb. mushrooms, sliced   (parsley, thyme and bay leaf)
6 or 8 scallions or shallots,   Herb croutons
   sliced, including part   (with parsley and tarragon)
   of the green tops

Brown steak lightly in butter, then mushrooms and scallions. Add wine, stock and bouquet garni. Cover tightly and simmer on low flame until tender—or transfer contents of skillet to a buttered casserole, cover and bake at 325°. When serving, sprinkle with herb croutons on top. (see Chap. IX)

A slightly different, but equally delicious, flavor may be obtained by substituting dry vermouth for the usual white wine. Since vermouth itself is very aromatic, with at least 16 different herbs, the bouquet garni should be omitted.

BRAISED ELK OR MOOSE STEAK

Sear a thick round steak in drippings, season with salt and freshly ground pepper, cover with dry red wine. Add 2 small onions studded with 2 cloves each, add parsnip, turnip and celery cut in small strips. Cover and simmer until tender and liquid is almost completely evaporated.

STROGANOFF

Stroganoff, as originally created, requires the choicest cuts from the tenderloin or rib. However, I prefer to save those cuts for broiling or roasting and have evolved this recipe using the less tender cuts.

2½ lbs. round steak

Combine: ½ cup flour, 1 tsp. salt, ½ tsp. ground pepper

½ cup butter	½ lb. mushrooms,
1 onion	sautéed briefly in
2 cups beef bouillon or game stock	¼ cup butter

Blend: 1 cup sour cream, ¼ cup tomato paste, 1 tsp. Worcestershire sauce

Finely chopped parsley

   While still partially frozen, remove tendons, bone and connective tissue from steak and cut into thin strips. (This is easier to do when the meat is still firm.) Coat strips of meat with seasoned flour. Heat butter in large skillet with tight fitting lid. Brown meat slowly, turning with tongs to brown all sides, ⅓ at a time. When meat is nearly all browned, add chopped onion and cook another 2 minutes. Slowly add bouillon, scraping skillet to loosen any browned particles. Cover tightly and simmer on very low flame until meat is tender. 10 minutes before serving add sautéed mushrooms and then sour cream mixture in small amounts, stirring vigorously. When all is well blended, continue cooking over low flame 5 minutes. Serve in preheated dish, garnished with chopped parsley. It is traditional to serve this dish with rice, but noodles may be used. (This is excellent party fare, by the way.)

STROGANOFF

*Saffron rice, peas with toasted almonds,
and stroganoff, savory with sour cream
and mushrooms — all the ingredients
for a colorful and delicious buffet
supper. Just be sure to have an extra
supply waiting in the kitchen — you'll
need it!*

SPICY SWISS STEAK

If you're tired of the usual Swiss steak, try this one—the flavor is subtle, despite the many ingredients.

Boned round or chuck steak
  1″ thick, cut in
  serving portions
¼ cup flour
4 whole cloves
Generous pinch marjoram or
  thyme
4 or 5 juniper berries

2 tsp. salt
Generous sprinkle coarsely
  ground black pepper
¼ tsp. ground ginger
Butter
1 small clove garlic, split
Beef bouillon or game stock

Combine flour, herbs and seasonings and crush together, using mortar and pestle. Pound seasoned flour into steak on both sides with edge of plate or back of cleaver. Melt butter in heavy skillet which has a tight fitting lid, add garlic and cook for a minute or so. Remove garlic and brown steak on both sides. Add enough stock to cover bottom of pan. Cover tightly and simmer until tender, adding more stock if necessary.

ORIENTAL PEPPER STEAK

This is, to a certain extent, a misnomer, since the orientals cook both meat and vegetables only a very short time. This compromise has two advantages—you can save the prime steak the orientals would use here and have a pleasant variation, not only for the cook, but for the diners as well.

2 lbs. round steak
½ cup butter
Dash of garlic salt
  or 1 small clove of garlic,
  minced
Dash of powdered ginger
½ cup soy sauce

1 cup beef bouillon
3 green peppers, sliced in strips
5 or 6 scallions, including
  the green tops, sliced
Salt and pepper
3 to 4 tbsps. cornstarch
½ cup white wine or water

Remove all tendons and connective tissue and slice steak into thin strips while the meat is still partially frozen. Cook over medium flame in butter with garlic and ginger until well browned. Add soy sauce and bouillon, cover and simmer until tender. Add green pepper and scallions, cook only a minute or so. Add cornstarch mixed with wine or water and stir on low flame until sauce is clear and thickened. Check seasonings—you may not need any salt and pepper. Serve with rice or crisp Chinese noodles.

BOAR CHOPS

Brown chops slowly in skillet, season with salt and pepper. Place in greased casserole, cover each chop with raw cranberry relish (see Chap. IX), cover casserole and bake at 350° at least 1½ hours or until tender. Add a bit of orange juice if needed near the end of the baking time.

 ## ITALIAN SCALOPPINE

2 lbs. boned round steak, cut in serving portions	Salt and pepper
4 tbsps. olive oil	1 tsp. dried parsley
1 clove garlic	
3 cups canned tomatoes, sieved, or tomato puree	
1 tsp. oregano	

Brown steak in oil with garlic, add tomato and seasonings. Cover and simmer until fork tender. If desired, a slice of Mozzarella cheese may be placed atop each portion and slid into the oven until cheese is melted.

BEAR STEAK

Cut a thick steak, sear under high flame on both sides. Then broil slowly until well done about 3″ from flame. About ½ hour is required for this operation. Serve with the following sauce:

1 onion, thinly sliced	Bouquet of: bay leaf, parsley, celery tops
½ lb. mushrooms, sliced	Pinch garlic powder
1 green pepper, sliced	2 cloves
Butter	1 tsp. meat glaze
1 cup dry red wine	
½ cup water	

Saute onion, mushrooms and pepper in small amount of butter for 5 minutes—do not brown. Add remaining ingredients and simmer 20 to 25 minutes. Remove herbs, season to taste with salt, blend in 1 glass currant jelly.

I am grateful to Mrs. G. C. F. Dalziel of Watson Lake, Yukon and the publishers of *The Whitehorse Star* for permission to include some of her recipes originally published in *The Whitehorse Star*, Whitehorse, Yukon.

 BRISKET

"Most people, if you offer them meat, want a 'Steak'—that is fine with me, but don't give away the brisket: no finer meal comes off the animal than this. Cut the brisket in fist-size hunks, dredge with flour and place in dutch oven sizzling hot with kidney fat and brown. Fresh ground pepper and salt and cover with water. Cover and simmer all afternoon, add vegetables and dumplings."

MOOSE CHOP SUEY

"Slice long thin strips of moose tenderloin, dump in paper bag with a cup of flour, shake in bag till coated with flour, brown till golden in fat. Thoroughly drain tin of whole mushrooms (saving broth till later) and brown mushrooms with meat, add a finely chopped spanish onion, a cup of finely chopped cabbage, a half cup diced celery and a tin of bean sprouts and let simmer for half hour, using mushroom broth if liquid gets too low in the pan. Mix two tablespoons corn starch with enough soy sauce to make a paste and add to mixture to thicken.

To serve, place in large platter, sprinkle with sesame seeds, and surround with white fluffy rice."

RIBS

Ribs very seldom last beyond the time spent in camp—this is only fitting and proper. They are at their best cut in sections, propped over a good bed of coals and broiled as is, or basted with a simple sauce, such as Barney's Barbecue sauce. (see Chap. X.)

If you are fortunate enough to have the ribs reach home, use them as soon as possible—they do take a fair bit of freezer space.

BAKED RIBS WITH BARBECUE SAUCE

Place ribs in large roasting pan, cover with barbecue sauce. (see Chap. X) Cover roaster and bake at 350° for 1½ hours, turning and basting several times.

BAKED BOAR RIBS WITH SAUERKRAUT

In roaster, place sauerkraut, 2 or 3 strips of bacon diced, 2 apples sliced, and a liberal sprinkle of caraway seed. Place boar ribs on top, sprinkle with salt and pepper, and bake at 350° for 1½ hours. Scrub a few Idaho potatoes and toss those in the oven next to the roaster the last 45 minutes.

CHAPTER IV

What To Do With All That 'Burger?

I HAVE HEARD THAT LAMENT from hunters' wives a number of times the last few years. There are, unfortunately, some butchers who think only in terms of steaks and hamburgers. They may be rushed or completely indifferent and take the easiest way out by putting as much as possible through the meat grinder. The butchers are not wholly to blame, however. I have heard hunters say, "I don't care—just cut it up and freeze it for me!" Serves 'em right for not being more specific!

On the other hand, there *are* times when it is wise to have a good quantity of 'burger ground. If you have a venerable trophy animal on your hands, grinding the less tender cuts may be the ideal solution.

The only trouble is that ground meat has a storage life of only 4 to 6 months in the freezer, and the cook may be hard pressed for new and different ways to get rid of it all before the family rebels.

The answer is simple: be a United Nations cook and invite your friends to share the feasts with you. The lowly 'burger can be prepared in literally hundreds of delicious ways.

Italian Dishes

The basis of many of the Italian dishes is the tomato sauce, which I prepare in huge quantities and freeze in quart containers. One word of warning, however: if you use plastic freezer containers for tomato sauce, you will find it almost impossible to reuse them for anything else —the tomato not only stains them, but the pungency of the sauce seems to permeate the plastic. Waxed tubs are the answer to this problem.

ITALIAN TOMATO SAUCE

3 onions, chopped	2 tsp. ground black pepper
3 #2 cans Italian plum tomatoes	2 tbsp. sugar

2 #2 cans tomato puree
6 6-oz. cans Italian tomato paste
4 cups water
1 to 2 tbsp. salt

3 to 4 bay leaves or
Generous sprinkle of basil
    and oregano
½ cup olive oil

Brown onions in olive oil, add remaining ingredients to large kettle, using water to rinse out the tomato paste cans. Cook over very low flame for about 2½ hours, stirring occasionally as it may tend to scorch. Cool, package and freeze. This will make 4 quarts of sauce.

MEAT BALLS

3 lbs. ground game meat
¾ lb. ground pork
2½ cups fine dry bread crumbs
1½ cups grated Parmesan
    or Romano cheese
8 to 10 sprigs fresh parsley,
    chopped or 3 tbsp. dried
    parsley flakes

2 cloves garlic, finely minced
1½ cups milk
6 eggs
Salt and pepper to taste

In large mixing bowl, beat eggs with milk, add bread crumbs, cheese, garlic, parsley, salt and pepper..Place meats in the bowl, roll up your sleeves and start mixing with your hands. It's the only way I've found to be certain the ingredients will all be thoroughly mixed, especially working with such large quantities. Set out a large skillet, form balls about the size of golf balls and brown on all sides in hot oil. As the balls are browned, set aside on a large platter to cool, if not to be used the same day. When cool, place on waxed paper covered cookie sheets and freeze. The individually frozen meat balls may be packaged in plastic sacks or containers. The advantage, of course, is that you can always remove just the quantity needed for a twosome or a crowd. The meat balls do need further cooking in the sauce before they are served: 20 minutes for thawed or unfrozen ones, at least ½ hour if frozen ones are dropped into the simmering sauce. A 1 lb. package of spaghetti, 2 quarts of the sauce, and half the meat balls in this recipe will serve 8 to 12 people, depending on their appetites.

Quick Variations on the Main Theme

1. For each quart of sauce, brown ½ to 1 lb. ground game in small amount of oil, breaking it into fairly small pieces as it browns. Add

ITALIAN SPAGHETTI AND MEAT BALLS

*Unexpected guests for dinner? No need
to be flustered when you have this
dinner waiting in your freezer. This
is one of our favorites and is served
often by "popular demand."*

thawed sauce and simmer until very hot.

2. Add ½ lb. sautéed mushrooms to 1 quart of sauce, along with ½ lb. browned 'burger.

3. Combine equal amounts of hot Italian sausage, browned and then cut in 1½″ pieces, and meat balls, and heat 20 minutes in the sauce.

LASAGNE

I usually double this recipe and make an extra casserole to freeze. To keep my casserole dishes in circulation, I line the casserole to be frozen with aluminum foil, freeze the lasagne and then remove the contents from the casserole and place it in a plastic bag. When I am ready to bake it, I peel the foil from the frozen lasagne, replace it in the casserole and bake it, allowing extra time in the oven if the food is not completely thawed.

1 quart tomato sauce
1½ lbs. game 'burger browned
    in small amount of oil
1 lb. broad lasagne noodles,
    cooked until barely tender
6 tbsp. Parmesan cheese

Ground black pepper
¾ lb. Mozzarella cheese, sliced
½ lb. Ricotta cheese (cottage
    cheese, drained, may be
    used)

In a deep casserole about 10″ by 6″, layer the ingredients as follows: Enough tomato sauce to cover the bottom of the casserole, 1 layer of noodles, ½ the total of Mozzarella cheese, ½ the ground meat, 3 tbsps. Parmesan, sprinkled evenly over the meat, generous sprinkle pepper, ½ the Ricotta.

Repeat the layering, adding the final layer of noodles on top and covering the noodles with additional sauce. Bake at 350° until bubbling (about ½ hour). Serve cut in squares with any sauce not used in the casserole.

ITALIAN STUFFED VEGETABLES

The following mixture may be used to stuff peppers, onions, or zucchini squash.
Stuffing:
1 lb. ground 'burger
½ cup cooked rice
2 tbsps. drippings

1 onion, chopped
    Salt and pepper to taste

Brown onion and 'burger in drippings for 5 minutes. Combine with the rice and seasonings, stuff parboiled vegetables, and place in greased casserole. Pour over and around the vegetables 1½ cups tomato sauce blended with ¼ cup water. Top the vegetables with slices of Mozzarella cheese. Bake at 325° for 20 to 25 minutes. Sufficient stuffing for 4 to 5 peppers, 6 to 8 onions, or 3 medium squash.

To parboil vegetables:

Peppers: cut off stem end, remove seeds and white membrane, boil in salted water 5 minutes, rinse in cold water, drain.

Onions: peel, cut off root end, as well as a slice from the top, boil in salted water 10 or 15 minutes, scoop out centers, leaving only the 3 outer layers.

Zucchini squash: cut off stem and blossom ends, scoop out seeds after splitting squash lengthwise, boil in salted water 5 to 8 minutes. It is not necessary to peel squash if they are young.

Scandinavian Dishes

MEAT BALLS

1 lb. 'burger
½ lb. ground pork
1 onion, chopped (may be
    omitted)
½ cup dry bread crumbs
½ cup milk
1 egg
1 tsp. salt
1 tsp. sugar

¼ tsp. each: nutmeg, cloves,
    ginger
½ tsp. allspice
2 tbsps. butter

Beat egg in milk, add crumbs and seasonings and blend well. Add meats and onion, if desired, mix thoroughly and shape into balls. If the meat balls are to be served at a buffet dinner, make them small—if they are to be used as a main dish, make them larger. Melt butter in large skillet, brown meat balls on all sides and cook thoroughly. Remove to a hot platter while you make the sauce.

Sauce:

3 tbsps. flour
    Salt and pepper to taste

2 cups top milk or
1 cup bouillon and 1 cup cream

Blend flour into fat in the skillet, slowly stir in liquid, blending on low flame until mixture thickens—do not boil. Check seasonings and pour sauce over meat balls.

For a flavor variation, equally Scandinavian, omit sugar, allspice, cloves and ginger from meat balls and substitute pepper to taste. Serve with sauce made as above with top milk, adding 2 tbsp. finely chopped fresh dill.

GAME PATTIES A LA LINDSTROM

1½ lbs. 'burger	1 egg, well beaten
1 lb. potatoes, boiled,	1 tbsp. minced onion
peeled and diced fine	2 tbsp. minced capers
¼ cup finely diced pickled beets	Salt and pepper to taste

Combine meat, egg, seasonings, onion and capers—mix well. Add diced potatoes and beets. If mixture seems too dry, add 1 or 2 tbsps. beet juice. Set in refrigerator for an hour before cooking to permit flavors to blend. Shape into thick patties and brown thoroughly on each side in buttered skillet.

South of the Border

CHILI CON CARNE CON FRIJOLES

2 lbs. frijoles or garbanzo beans	3 finely chopped garlic cloves
¼ lb. bacon, diced	1 8-oz. can tomato sauce
4 to 5 onions, sliced	Salt and pepper
3 lbs. 'burger or chuck	Chili powder to taste—
cut in 1" cubes	start with 2 or 3 tbsps. and
1 quart canned or fresh	work your way up
peeled tomatoes, chopped	

Soak the beans overnight in cold water, then drain and cook in water or stock until tender. Drain and set aside. Cook bacon in large kettle until crisp. Remove crisp bits and reserve. Brown meat, onions and 2 tbsp. of chili powder in the bacon fat. Add tomatoes and sauce, garlic, salt and pepper and additional chili powder to taste. Simmer at least ½ hour to allow flavors to blend (if using cubed chuck, until meat is tender). Add cooked beans, simmer 20 minutes longer. This makes enough for a large group—15 to 20 people—but since it does freeze well, it's just as easy to make a large amount. When reheating frozen chili, check the seasoning again—I have sometimes found it necessary to add more seasoning.

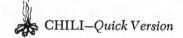

CHILI—*Quick Version*

The Mexicans would not approve of this at all, but it does make a good camp dish—I have used it at home in emergencies too, for it takes only ½ hour from freezer to table.

4 tbsps. butter or drippings   Chili powder to taste
1 lb. 'burger
2 sliced onions
1 shredded green pepper,
    if desired
2 15-oz. cans Mexican beans
    in chili gravy

Brown meat and onions in fat (start with frozen meat if necessary), breaking the meat in small pieces as it browns. Add green pepper and chili beans. Cover and simmer 10 minutes, check seasoning, add more chili powder if desired and simmer 10 minutes more.

MEXICAN MEAT BALLS IN SAUCE

1½ lbs. 'burger   1 garlic clove, minced
6 tbsps. corn meal   2 tsps. curry powder
1 egg plus 1 egg yolk, beaten   (or cumin, if available)
1 onion, chopped   Salt and pepper

Combine all ingredients and shape into small balls. Cook for 10 minutes in the following sauce:

2 tbsps. butter   Chili powder
1 onion, chopped   1 quart V-8 or tomato juice
1 green pepper, chopped

Cook onion and green pepper in melted butter until lightly browned, add juice and season to taste with chili powder. Simmer for 10 minutes and then add meat balls.

ARROZ CON CARNE

It is doubtful whether the Mexicans or Spaniards had anything to do with this one—but we enjoy it nevertheless.

4 tbsps. oil or drippings
1 cup raw long grain rice
1 onion, chopped
1 to 1½ lbs. 'burger
1 green pepper, chopped

Pinch of garlic powder,
    if desired
1 tbsp. chili powder
1 quart canned tomatoes
½ cup sliced olives,
    black or green

Brown rice, onion and meat in hot oil in a large skillet. Add remaining ingredients, stir well, cover tightly and simmer over very low flame until rice is tender (about 45 minutes). If mixture appears to be getting dry, add a few spoons of tomato liquid or water, but do not stir.

TAMALE PIE

Very few of us have the time or the ingredients, such as corn husks and the freshly ground Mexican corn meal, to make real tamales. This recipe might be called a Gringo adaptation.

Crust:
1 cup yellow corn meal
2 large eggs

¼ cup water
Salt and pepper

Beat eggs with water, stir in corn meal vigorously and season to taste. Let the mixture stand while preparing the filling.

Filling:
Butter or oil
2 onions, thinly sliced
2 cups tomato puree
1 green pepper, chopped

1 tbsp. chili powder
1 lb. ground game meat
1 cup canned or frozen corn
Pinch of garlic powder

Brown meat, onions and pepper in hot oil. Add remaining ingredients and simmer for 10 minutes, stirring once or twice. Grease a 2 quart casserole and while the filling is simmering, pat out crust on a sheet of waxed paper to conform with the shape of the casserole. Pour in the hot filling, flip the crust on top and bake in a preheated oven at 425° until the crust is browned.

Eastern European Dishes

There are countless variations of these old European dishes and their original origins have become lost as each cook adds or substitutes ingredients at hand. You may have different ways of preparing them, but the end result is hearty and delicious on a cold winter evening.

CABBAGE CASSEROLE

1 head cabbage, shredded
1 lb. ground game
2 or 3 stalks celery, chopped
1 green pepper, chopped
3 tart apples, pared,
   cored and sliced

3 cups canned tomatoes
1 bay leaf
   Pinch of cloves (or garlic
     powder)
   Salt and pepper to taste

Remove outer leaves from cabbage, wash and shred. Let the cabbage drain while you brown the meat, celery and pepper in a small amount of hot fat. Remove from the flame, add cabbage, apple slices, tomatoes and seasonings. Mix all together thoroughly and turn into covered casserole. Bake in a slow oven 275° to 300° for 1½ hours.

STUFFED CABBAGE LEAVES

The Armenians use grape leaves for another variation of this dish.

1 large head of cabbage
1½ lbs. ground game
1 onion, chopped
1 egg
1 tbsp. salt
1 tsp. pepper
1 tbsp. paprika
1 cup raw rice

4 cups canned tomatoes,
   cut in pieces
1 sliced onion
1 bay leaf
1 cup sour cream

Remove the core and any wilted outer leaves from the cabbage. Place in boiling salted water for 5 to 10 minutes to soften the leaves. Remove each leaf whole and set aside to drain. Combine meat, onion, beaten egg, seasonings and rice—mix well. On each cabbage leaf, place 2 or 3 tbsps. filling, fold the sides of the leaf over and roll up.

It may be necessary to remove part of the heavy rib on some of the larger leaves so they will roll more easily. Tie each roll with white string and set aside. Grease a large casserole, place in the bottom the remainder of the cabbage, shredded, onion and bay leaf. Set the cabbage rolls on top and pour over the canned tomatoes. Cover the casserole and bake at 350° until the cabbage rolls are very tender— allow 1 to 1½ hours. Add the sour cream, scalded, and serve with dark bread.

In the Near East, this same recipe is used with lamb or mutton—if you have goat or sheep meat available, try it in this recipe in place of the venisonburger.

Just 'Burgers

Hamburgers are so much a part of the American diet that we forget that their origin was in Hamburg, Germany. The original Hamburger steak was quite different from the ground meat patty we know today. However, thick or thin, broiled or pan fried, rare or well done, they can still be varied considerably with a bit of imagination.

MIXED GRILL

Our antelope 'burger was so superb this past year that it deserved rather special treatment. This definitely takes 'burgers out of the prosaic class. For each serving, prepare:

1 medium sized 'burger, wrapped 'round with bacon and skewered
1 or 2 large stuffed mushroom caps (see Chap. XIII)
½ beefsteak tomato, sprinkled with buttered crumbs and oregano
1 large pork sausage

Start 'burger and sausage first, about 3" from the broiler flame. After 5 to 8 minutes, add tomato and mushroom—turn the meats and broil an additional 5 to 8 minutes.

Other 'Burger Suggestions

1. Instead of the usual fried onions, blend equal amounts of blue cheese and butter, place 2 tsps. on each patty when they are done.

Turn off broiler and leave in the oven just long enough to melt the topping—while you serve up the vegetables.

2. If 'burgers are pan fried, remove them to a hot platter, blend into pan juices a small amount of any canned or dehydrated soup you prefer—could be mushroom, celery, or onion. Stir in water or milk and allow to come to a boil, stirring and scraping pan. Simmer for several minutes until gravy is smooth and pour over the meat patties.

3. ½ cup sour cream, blended with 1 tbsp. flour, stirred into pan juices with 1 tbsp. capers and a pinch of dried minced onion. Stir until thick and smooth, but do not boil.

4. Heat a cup or so of Creole sauce (see Chap. X) while 'burgers are broiling. Pour over and serve.

MEAT LOAF

The possibilities for variation are endless on meat loaf too. These are our favorites, which I could make blindfolded by now. However, these are the ingredients as Mother wrote them down for me years ago.

BEEF LOAF

1½ lbs. ground beef (these
   days I use venison burger)
   or 1 lb. ground beef and
   ½ lb. sausage meat
2 eggs
1 cup milk
⅔ cup dry bread crumbs
½ onion, chopped
1 green pepper, chopped
1 tsp. salt

Generous grinding of black
   pepper
1 tsp. poultry seasoning,
   if sausage meat is not used

Beat eggs with milk, add crumbs and seasonings, onions and green pepper. Blend thoroughly with meat and place in greased loaf pan, pressing down thoroughly with fork. Place in preheated oven at 350° for 10 minutes, then spoon over chili sauce (see Chap. X) and bake for an additional 35 to 40 minutes, adding additional chili sauce if necessary. (If there is any left over, it can be wrapped in foil and frozen, to be reheated another day. It is equally good sliced cold for sandwiches.)

HAM LOAF

A good place to use some of the less tender portions of that wild boar.

1¼ lbs. ground fresh pork boar)	1 cup fine dry bread crumbs
¾ lb. ground smoked ham	6 tbsps. brown sugar, packed
2 eggs	2 to 3 tsps. dry mustard
1 cup milk	Generous sprinkle of ground black pepper

Beat eggs with milk, add bread crumbs and black pepper, mix well with ground meats and pack firmly into greased loaf pan. Mix brown sugar and dry mustard together, add a few drops of water or fruit juice, just enough to form a thick paste. Spread on top of the ham loaf and bake until well done at 350°—about 1 hour. (When I have had more ham than pork on hand, I have altered the proportions of meat with no disastrous results.)

Or try it this way:

1. Add leftover cooked vegetables to the beef loaf.
2. When reheating beef loaf, frost with leftover mashed potatoes, beaten fluffy again with an egg and a bit of milk. Grated sharp cheese makes a nice addition to the potatoes also.
3. Bake in loaf shape in an open flat pan—after 10 or 15 minutes, long enough for the crust to set, baste with canned soup of your choice —or criss cross with bacon slices.
4. Bake ham loaf in greased muffin cups 45 minutes—turn out onto broiled pineapple slices. This is attractive for a buffet supper.

Casseroles for Company

BRYN MAWR CASSEROLE

I was introduced to this delectable one at a Chicago Bryn Mawr Club luncheon. It is an Americanized version of lasagne—one well worth remembering when serving a large group of people.

¾ lb. noodles, cooked, drained and rinsed	1 lb. cottage cheese
	½ cup sour cream

2 tbsp. butter
2 lbs. ground chuck (any member
    of the deer family)
4 8-oz. cans tomato sauce
1 tsp. salt
    Dash of Worcestershire sauce

2 8-oz. packages cream cheese
    at room temperature
2 tbsps. chopped green pepper
2 tbsps. melted butter
½ cup minced scallions

Brown meat in butter, drain off any excess fat, stir in tomato sauce, salt and Worcestershire sauce. Blend the cream cheese and cottage cheese with sour cream, add green pepper, and ½ the minced scallions. Mix the noodles and cheese blend together and place in the bottom of a large flat casserole, which has been well buttered. Spread the meat and tomato mixture on top of the noodles and sprinkle with the reserved scallions which have been tossed with the two tbsps. melted butter. Bake at 350° for 30 to 45 minutes, depending on the depth of the casserole. This amount serves 8 people generously.

GRAND LAMB CASSEROLE

2 tbsps. butter
2 lbs. ground lamb or sheep
¼ cup minced onion
1 green pepper, chopped
1 egg
1 cup sour cream

3 tbsps. chopped parsley
    Salt and pepper to taste
    Generous sprinkle of marjoram
1 cup coarsely shredded carrot
½ cup finely minced celery

Brown lamb or sheep in butter, breaking into small pieces. Add onion and green pepper and continue cooking for another 2 or 3 minutes. Remove from flame, add egg beaten with sour cream, seasonings and parsley. Mix well and pour half of mixture into a greased two quart casserole. Blend carrot and celery together and sprinkle evenly over meat. Add rest of meat and bake at 350°. After 30 minutes, top with previously baked wedges of sesame seed pastry (see Chap. XI) and continue to bake for an additional 15 minutes. Serves 6.

PORCUPINE CASSEROLE

I recall being fascinated with this dish as a child. We've had fun with it lately at informal suppers. Bob will ask casually in front of our guests, "Say, what's for supper?" When I answer just as casually, "Oh, I thought we'd try the porcupines tonight," you can imagine the reactions we get, especially among the uninitiated!

1½ lbs. 'burger	⅔ cup raw long grain rice
1 onion, chopped	Salt and pepper to taste
1 egg	1 cup V-8 juice
¼ cup milk	½ cup chili sauce
½ cup bread crumbs	

Beat egg with milk, add bread crumbs, rice and meat. Season to taste and form into good sized meat balls. Place in a buttered casserole, pour over combined V-8 and chili sauce, and bake uncovered at 350° for 1 to 1½ hours, depending on the size of the meat balls. Baste occasionally with the liquid, adding more if it seems necessary.

CHAPTER V

Birds

WRITING THIS CHAPTER brings back a flood of memories, for bird shooting was my introduction to hunting. Our constant hunting companion in those days was deadly with his Browning O/U and his springer (the sire of our dog) was equally fabulous. We were training a new hunter as well as a young pup, so nearly every weekend was spent afield from the time the shooting preserves opened in early fall. We tried valiantly not to be outdone by this pair of "hunting fools" who would rather hunt than eat—as a consequence the portable cooler was always pretty well filled when we returned home.

Golden's Bridge, New York, for pheasants—and the thrill of the first pheasant I ever bagged—the hills of Hunterdon County, New Jersey, for rabbit and grouse—Wading River along the Jersey shore for ducks. . . .

Until we acquired a freezer, birds were practically every-day fare in our house. I soon learned to present them in different ways to avoid a clamor for hot dogs as a change of pace.

Wild birds, in contrast to their domestic cousins, are lean and need to be covered with bacon or larding pork and basted frequently to prevent drying of their delectable meat. As with any meat or fowl, the young are broiled or roasted, the elders are braised or fricasseed. The best indication of age is the breastbone—if the tip is soft and pliable, you have a young one, if the breastbone is rigid, you have to use a different culinary approach. When roasting or broiling, be certain that the oven is thoroughly preheated—this is particularly important with the tiny birds which require only a brief cooking period under intense heat. These luscious morsels should always be served with croutons or crisp trenchers of bread to soak up every last drop of goodness.

The various combinations of flavors in the recipes I have given are not necessarily limited to one particular species of bird. They may be used successfully with a variety of birds—only the amounts given and the cooking time will vary with the size and species of bird.

Upland Birds

Included in this classification are crow, dove, grouse, partridge, pigeon, pheasant, quail, turkey and woodcock.

Crow

The less said about these pesky birds the better, including the worn-out phrase "to eat crow"!! These black robbers are fine targets for the gunner during the off-season and I approve of them being shot—they cause so much damage. I do *not* approve of them in my kitchen, although I understand the young ones are quite edible, if parboiled. If I were in dire straits, I'd certainly look for a more tasty target for my last shell.

Doves and Pigeons

Dove and pigeon shooting can be a most humbling experience, so if your mighty hunter brings home doves or pigeons, treat them with all due respect—and *don't* ask about the shotshell consumption! The mourning dove is protected in some states as a song bird, but where it is legal game, it is considered excellent for the table, along with the white-winged dove and the band-tailed pigeon. Their diet consists mainly of grains and the various legumes—occasionally the flesh may be bitter if the birds have been feeding extensively on acorns.

The young, known as squab, are recognized by their light red breast meat and plump legs—they are best roasted, with one bird per serving. Darker breast meat and scrawny legs indicates a bird for stew or casserole.

ROAST SQUAB

Rub the birds with lemon juice, stuff with rice and raisin stuffing II (see Chap. X), truss and season lightly with salt and pepper. Spread the birds liberally with softened (not melted) butter and roast covered for 1 hour in a preheated 300° oven. Baste the birds frequently with hot water and additional butter. Garnish with watercress.

An alternate method of roasting squab is to wrap the seasoned and stuffed birds in bacon slices (but go easy on the salt) and roast at

425° for 25 to 30 minutes. Remove the bacon slices when the birds are almost done, allowing the breasts to brown. Be sure to baste with the pan juices during this time, so the meat does not dry out.

BRAISED PIGEONS IN ITALIAN SAUCE

In a flame proof casserole, brown older birds in butter, being sure all sides are attractively browned. Season lightly, add Italian Sauce (see Chap. X), cover casserole tightly and simmer on low flame until tender.

BREAST OF PIGEON WITH WINE SAUCE

This is suitable for larger pigeons.

Lift and cut away the skin from the breast. With a sharp boning knife, remove the breast filets by cutting down each side of the breastbone. Allow the two filets from each bird for one serving. Reserve the remainder of the carcass for soup, pâté or perhaps a Brunswick stew (see Chap. VI). Marinate the breasts for 1 hour in red or white wine to cover, with 1 tsp. lemon juice added. Drain filets and reserve marinade. Season the filets and sauté gently in butter until tender. Meanwhile, reduce the marinade by half in a small saucepan and add ¼ cup currant jelly, 1 tbsp. orange juice concentrate, and some finely shredded orange peel. Simmer for several minutes and serve the breasts on crisp croutons cut to the same size, with the sauce poured over. Braised celery would be delicious with this dish.

DOVES EN CASSEROLE

4 older doves	Several sprigs parsley and
¼ cup butter	thyme, chopped
1 oz. dried Italian mushrooms,	½ cup dry sherry
broken in small pieces	2 cups game bird stock
½ onion, minced	½ cup sliced stuffed olives
1 tbsp. flour	Salt and pepper to taste

Brown birds on all sides in skillet in hot butter, season lightly and remove to a casserole. In the same butter, brown onion, herbs and mushrooms for 5 minutes, add flour and stir until it too is slightly brown and bubbly. Lower flame, add stock and stir until sauce is smooth. Add sherry and olives, simmer an additional minute or so and check seasoning. Pour sauce into casserole, cover and bake at 350° until tender—about 45 minutes.

Grouse

With all the common names which vary and overlap from one section of the country to another, the matter of terminology can be rather confusing, especially when you get into the sub-species. There are six main varieties of grouse found in North America:

1. Ruffed grouse—the white fleshed boomer of the woodlands and slashings, one of our most delicious game birds, weighs up to 2 lbs.
2. Spruce grouse—as its name implies, a dweller of the northern spruce forests.
3. Blue or dusky grouse—found in the western pine forests, weighs up to 3½ lbs.
4. Pinnated grouse—larger and heavier than the ruffed grouse, a lover of the wide open spaces, hence his common name of prairie chicken.
5. Sharp-tailed grouse—a bit larger than the pinnated grouse, also prefers the prairies, but ranges farther north than the pinnated grouse.
6. Sage grouse—largest of all the grouse family, weighs up to 8 lbs., as implied by their name their diet consists primarily of sage tips, only the young birds are to be considered palatable since they depend less on the sage and more on insects and grains.

I have also included under this heading the willow and rock ptarmigan, a close relative of the Scottish red grouse, found in the northernmost parts of the continent.

ROAST GROUSE

Depending on their size, a grouse will serve 1 to 2 people. Other recipes suitable for grouse will be found under quail, partridge and pheasant.

Using the grouse livers, prepare rice stuffing I (see Chap. X). Stuff the birds lightly and truss. Cover the breasts with larding pork and roast on a rack with enough game bird stock to just cover the bottom of the roasting pan. Roast in an oven preheated to 450° for 15 minutes, reduce heat to 300° and continue to roast covered for 25 to 30 minutes, basting at least twice with the pan juices. Remove the larding strips, rub with butter and dust very lightly with flour. Then return to 400° oven to brown the skin (no more than a few minutes). Make gravy from the pan juices with roux and additional stock if necessary or serve with currant jelly and the traditional English bread sauce.

 BROILED GROUSE

Depending on their size, either split the birds in half or remove the backbone and breastbone and flatten the birds for broiling whole. Brush liberally with melted butter, season with salt and pepper. Broil over hot coals or in a preheated broiler for 10 minutes per side. Remove the birds to a heated platter and keep warm while you prepare Rouennaise from the grouse livers and the pan drippings from the broiled grouse. Spread Rouennaise on toasted buttery croutons and serve. (see Chap. IX for Rouennaise)

GROUSE ROASTED WITH PORT WINE

Sprinkle lightly inside and out with salt and pepper. Insert 1 tsp. butter inside each bird, wrap in bacon slices or larding pork. Place in open pan in preheated oven at 400° for 30 minutes, basting twice with additional butter. During the last 10 minutes of roasting time, add 1 glass of port wine and baste again. Serve with wild rice and gravy made from the pan juices.

ROAST GROUSE OR PARTRIDGE WITH ORANGE SLICES

Season the birds with salt and pepper, place an orange slice in the cavity of each bird. Wrap in bacon slices and roast in a 350° oven for 20 to 30 minutes, basting with the following ingredients several times:

Shredded orange peel
1 tbsp. orange juice concentrate
1 tsp. lemon juice
2 tbsp. water
4 tbsp. butter
   Combine all ingredients and

simmer for a minute or so to blend.

When birds are done, remove strings from birds and orange slices from the cavities. Serve on platter garnished with parsley and glazed orange slices (see Chap. IX).

BRAISED GROUSE—*Central European Style*

Also suitable for any older upland bird.

Stuff each bird with:

Its own liver   1 allspice berry
Celery leaves   Chunk of butter
1 juniper berry
Small sprig of thyme
Small strip of orange
  or lemon peel

Season the birds with salt and pepper, cover with bacon slices or larding pork. In a covered casserole, place a layer of chopped vegetables, including celery, carrot and onion. Barely cover the vegetables with an equal portion of stock and wine (white or red). Place the larded birds atop the vegetables, cover and braise in 400° oven until tender—the time, of course will depend on the size and age of the birds. Add additional wine and stock if necessary. When birds are tender, remove to a heated platter and keep warm, also take out stuffing from cavities. Strain the sauce from the casserole into a saucepan, bring to a boil, add ½ cup cream and heat just to the boiling point.

SMOTHERED GROUSE OR PTARMIGAN

Split the grouse or ptarmigan in half, roll in flour which has been seasoned with salt, pepper and thyme. Brown in hot butter, along with mushroom caps. When all is delicately browned, pour over enough heated heavy cream to half cover the birds. Cover tightly and bake at 350° until the birds are tender—about an hour for older birds.

The above recipe is not limited to the kitchen—as any good "substitute" cook knows. When the birds are browned, add a foil package of dehydrated cream of mushroom soup which has been thinned to the consistency of cream with water and/or evaporated milk. Cover and set over a slow fire in your trusty dutch oven.

GROUSE ALLA MILANO

"It's different, but delicious—What is it?" If you've never used fennel seed in cooking before, do try it! Fennel seed is faintly reminiscent of anise and is used not only in Italian cooking, but in Scandinavian dishes as well.

2 or 3 grouse, depending on size
   Flour, seasoned with
      salt and pepper
4 tbsps. butter or olive oil
2 or 3 scallions,
   finely sliced, including
   part of the green tops
1 cup game bird or chicken stock

1½ pkgs. frozen green peas or
   the equivalent in fresh ones
½ tsp. fennel seeds
1 tbsp. lemon juice
   Roux, if necessary

Cut grouse in serving portions, coat with seasoned flour, brown in hot fat along with scallions. Lower heat, add stock, cover and simmer until tender. Add peas, fennel seed and lemon juice, continue to simmer 10 minutes more. Check seasonings. If gravy does not seem thick enough, add small amount of roux and blend well. Serve with fluffy rice and a green salad.

Partridge

All nicknames to the contrary, there are only two true partridges in this country, both are fairly recent imports. One is the Chukar from the region around the Himalayas, closely related to the red-legged or French partridge. The other is the Hun or European grey partridge. The grey is found in the British Isles as well as on the Continent; however, since most of the birds transplanted here came from Hungary, the name Hun has stuck. Partridge is considered a great delicacy by gourmets everywhere and each 10 to 14 oz. bird is sufficient for one serving.

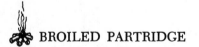 BROILED PARTRIDGE

If you are fortunate enough to bag a few of these birds as an added bonus on a big game trip, they are most delicious broiled over the coals of an open fire.

Season inside and out with a light sprinkle of salt and pepper, add a small chunk of butter to the cavity along with the bird's own liver with a pinch of thyme or dried onion flakes. Wrap the birds well in bacon strips and skewer. Truss securely on a spit and broil slowly over coals, turning to brown all sides evenly. It's worth a bit of extra effort to construct a drip pan of heavy foil and place it directly under the bird to catch all the succulent juices that drip from the bird as it broils. Prepare crisp slices of toast, soak in the pan juices, add the livers which have been cooking inside the birds, put the birds on top—and who needs Escoffier?

BRAISED PARTRIDGE—*Chasseur*

This old European classic, although designated as "hunter's style", seemed destined to be prepared at home exclusively, until the advent of the dehydrated and freeze-dried foods. Now those older birds can be prepared just as well in camp as in the kitchen. I'll list the original recipe first and then mention the adaptations.

Core and remove any wilted leaves from a good size head of cabbage. Parboil in salted water for 8 to 10 minutes, drain and remove 4 outer leaves whole for each bird to be braised. (Allow one bird per serving.) Shred the remainder of the cabbage and place in the bottom of an earthenware casserole. Brown the seasoned birds in butter or bacon fat, turning so all sides are evenly browned, then wrap each bird in the reserved cabbage leaves and tie securely. Place in the casserole along with 1 strip of bacon, diced, 2 sliced carrots and 1 juniper berry *per bird*. Boil up 2 cups of game bird stock in the pan the birds were browned in, add shredded lemon peel and scrape the pan, loosening any browned bits that adhere. Pour over the birds and vegetables, cover and place in 325° oven until birds are tender—about 45 minutes. Remove strings and serve birds in nests of cabbage with noodles and any tart or spicy jelly.

Brown the birds in bacon fat in the dutch oven. Set the birds aside while you add 2 chicken bouillon cubes and 2 cups water to the dutch oven. Let the water come to a boil while you stir until the bouillon cubes are dissolved. Add part of a package of dehydrated shredded cabbage, the same of carrots, a bit of dried minced onion and let it simmer for a couple of minutes. You may need to add more chicken broth at this time, plus a bit of salt. Toss in a few diced bacon strips, the browned birds, cover and set over a slow fire until the birds are tender. Check occasionally to see that there is enough liquid so the vegetables don't scorch—but don't drown them in liquid. The whole idea in this dish is that the vegetables steam along with the birds and add their savory goodness to the meat.

PARTRIDGE PATE

This recipe from a very old Viennese cook book uses, of course, the European grey partridge. An equivalent amount of quail or grouse may be substituted.

2 or 3 partridge
½ lb. bacon
10 whole peppercorns
1 glass dry white wine
1 large hard roll
4 whole eggs
1 egg yolk
   Salt and pepper to taste
1 goose liver, finely minced

½ lb. fresh mushrooms, finely minced

(since goose liver is not as readily available here, you may substitute 6 to 8 chicken livers plus 2 to 3 tbsps. melted butter)

Clean and wipe birds, wrap in bacon and place in covered casserole with whole peppercorns. Simmer over very low flame or in slow oven 275° until birds are tender. Add 1 glass white wine, simmer 10 additional minutes and allow birds to cool. Remove meat from the bones, break hard roll in several pieces and place in casserole to soak up the juices. Put partridge, bacon and roll through fine blade of the food chopper twice. Beat eggs and extra yolk thoroughly, add meat and bacon mixture and season to taste with salt and freshly ground pepper. Combine the chopped mushrooms and liver. (Do not prepare mushrooms until you are ready to use them, as they will darken.) Butter a mold liberally, pack in a layer of partridge, then some of the mushroom and liver mixture, and so on, ending with a layer of the partridge mixture. Cover mold with a layer of waxed paper and then one of heavy foil, tie securely and set on a rack in a kettle of boiling water. Cover kettle and steam 1 to 1½ hours. Serve cold with very thinly sliced hot buttered toast or watercress sandwiches.

PARTRIDGE EN CASSEROLE

This recipe is particularly suited to older birds; grouse and quail, as well as partridge.

Insert one juniper berry in the cavity of each bird, allowing one bird per serving (unless the larger grouse are used). Brown the birds in butter, season lightly with salt and pepper, place in casserole atop braising vegetables: equal amounts of chopped carrots, celery and onions. Add sufficient stock to cover the vegetables almost completely, add 1 pony of brandy, 1 bay leaf and a pinch of thyme and parsley. Place ½ lb. fresh sliced mushrooms around the birds, cover the casserole and place in 400° oven until birds are tender—the time will vary, naturally, with the age and size of the birds.

Pheasant

Although epicures insist that some of the tinier birds are superior in flavor, my favorite is still the majestic ringneck. Perhaps it's because his plumage is so beautiful to look at, as he cackles indignantly when flushed from the hedgerow. But "handsome is as handsome does" and he is equally enjoyable at the dinner table. The cocks weigh an average of 2½ to 4 lbs., hens about 2 to 3 lbs., so 2 or 3 servings per bird may be planned on.

PHEASANT AMANDINE

A recipe suitable for young birds.

Split each pheasant as you would a broiling chicken, season with pepper and a very scant sprinkle of salt, place bone side down in a roasting pan, cover with bacon slices, held in place with skewers. Roast in 350° oven, basting frequently with ¼ cup melted butter and pan juices until tender, about 1 hour. (When the age of the bird is in doubt, cover the birds with aluminum foil at mid-point in the roasting.) When the bird is tender, add ¼ cup melted butter, blended with 1 tbsp. lemon juice and ¼ cup blanched, slivered almonds. Return to oven for 10 minutes, basting once more. Serve with wild rice and spiced cranberry sauce.

I have achieved the same effect on an outdoor grill and served a rather elegant supper on the terrace. Place a square of butter in the rib section of each half, season and wrap in bacon. Wrap each portion in a double thickness of heavy aluminum foil and seal with the drug-store wrap fold so none of the juices will escape. Place over the coals and turn the packages carefully from time to time to permit the birds to cook evenly. I use very heavy mitts for this job, to prevent puncturing the foil. Open the packages the last few minutes to permit the bacon to crisp and, using a basting syringe, draw off the excess juices to add to the pan of almond lemon butter which has been waiting at the side of the grill. The wild rice has also been steaming covered on a slow part of the fire. Serve a green salad and reserve the cranberries for dessert, where they may appear as a frosty Cranberry sherbet or Cranberry Bavarian (see Chap. XV).

PHEASANT—*Spanish Style with Saffron Rice*

2 young pheasants, disjointed	6 tbsps. frozen orange
¼ cup butter	juice concentrate
Salt and pepper	1¼ cups game bird stock or
2 tbsp. flour	chicken bouillon
Dash of cloves	⅔ cup golden raisins
1 piece of stick cinnamon	⅔ cup shredded toasted almonds
Dash of Tabasco	

Brown the birds, cut in serving pieces, in melted butter in large covered skillet. Season with salt and pepper and set on plate when they are nicely browned. Blend into the butter in the skillet the flour and cloves. Stir until bubbly, then add the stock, orange juice concentrate and Tabasco and continue to stir and blend until thickened and boiling. Add the cinnamon and raisins and return the pheasant pieces to the sauce. Cover and simmer on low heat until tender—45 minutes or so. Just before serving, remove the piece of stick cinnamon and stir the almonds into the sauce. Serve the pheasant on a platter mounded with saffron rice (see Chap. XIII), pour some of the sauce on the birds, pass the rest in a sauce boat.

PHEASANT IN CREAM

Equally good for partridge or grouse.

Brown seasoned birds in a liberal amount of butter in a covered casserole or skillet on a moderate flame. Turn to brown all sides. Cover and let the birds simmer in their own juices over low heat until tender. Combine 1½ tbsps. roux and 1 cup cream, add a grating of fresh nutmeg, stir until smooth and pour over birds. Cook for an additional few minutes, basting the birds with the cream. Remove birds to Rouennaise covered croutons, blend sauce and pour over the birds.

If you enjoy a bit of crunch in the sauce, add celery which has been sliced on the diagonal and steamed in a small amount of water for 5 minutes—no longer!

PHEASANT VIENNESE STYLE

Suitable for any older bird.

Place pheasant in kettle, barely cover with water—about 1 quart. Add:

1 bay leaf	2 carrots, sliced
1 tbsp. salt	2 stalks celery, sliced
6 to 8 peppercorns	
1 medium onion, sliced	

Cover and simmer until pheasant is tender, about 2½ hours.

Remove pheasant, skin and remove meat from bones. Return bones to broth and reduce liquid by half. Strain broth. In double boiler top over low flame, combine and stir until bubbly but not browned:
½ cup butter
½ cup flour

Slowly add 2 cups pheasant broth, stir constantly until thick, then add:
1 cup thin cream

Place over boiling water, combine with the sauce and heat thoroughly:
½ tsp. freshly grated nutmeg
  Pheasant, cut in large dice
1 can white asparagus tips,
    drained
1 can mushrooms, drained
½ lemon, *very* thinly sliced

Serve over puff paste rounds.

ROAST PHEASANT

Season with salt and freshly ground pepper inside and out. Stuff the
cavity with any preferred stuffing (see Chap. X) or:

Bay leaf	Parsley sprigs
Slice of lemon	Slice of onion
Celery leaves	

Cook the liver and giblets in stock until tender and chop. Reserve
stock and giblets for gravy. Cover the pheasant with bacon strips and
place in roaster. Add sufficient stock and white wine (if desired) to
cover the bottom of the roasting pan. Cover and cook 1 hour at 350°
or until tender. Remove larding strips, return to oven uncovered to
permit skin to brown, basting every few minutes with juices in the pan.
Remove pheasant to heated platter (and remove celery and parsley
sprigs) while you prepare the gravy. Add roux to pan juices, stir
until well blended, then add giblets and giblet broth. Stir and scrape
sides of roaster, cook slowly until thickened, and pour into preheated
sauce boat.

BREAST OF PHEASANT ALLA MAMA LEONE

The inspiration for this dish came from Mama Leone's famous Italian
restaurant in New York. One evening while dining there with friends,
I tried Saltimbocca alla Romano, veal with Mozzarella cheese and
Prosciutto ham. The combination of flavors was most delicious, so the
next time we had an abundance of young pheasants I began experimenting. The result is this recipe—whether it bears any great resem-
blance to the original I do not know, but I'm certain you will enjoy
it nevertheless.

Allow one pheasant breast per person. Remove breasts whole,
reserving legs and carcass for a game pie. Bone each breast, starting at
the lower edge of the ribs and cutting as close as possible to the bone.
Be careful not to cut through the skin at the top of the breastbone.
Place each boned breast on a sheet of waxed paper, cover with another
and flatten slightly with the broad flat side of the cleaver. Season with
pepper and a pinch of thyme (no salt is necessary). Place on each
breast a slice of Mozzarella or Gruyère cheese, a slice of Prosciutto
or other thinly sliced ham, another slice of cheese, all slightly smaller

ROAST PHEASANT

*Spiced cranberry sauce, wild rice, and
mushroom caps are the background —
and a delicious one it is — for two
cocks that did not escape the patterns
of our shotguns. A festive feast for
four.*

in size than the breast when folded in half. Fold each breast in half and skewer or sew together. Brown in butter over a moderate flame and then transfer to a buttered baking dish and bake at 350° until tender—about ½ hour. Meanwhile, prepare the sauce by blending 2 or 3 tbsps. flour into the butter in which the breasts were browned, using a very moderate flame so the roux will remain a delicate color. Slowly blend in 1 cup game bird stock, stirring constantly so the sauce remains smooth. Add 1 cup cream and then cook, stirring constantly until the sauce is thickened. When the pheasant breasts are tender, place on a heated platter, blend into the sauce any juices in the baking dish and several tbsps. dry sherry or white wine. Check seasoning of the sauce and serve over the pheasant breasts.

PHEASANT HUNGARIAN STYLE

This adaptation of Paprika Huhn is equally good for young or older birds. The length of time for cooking will vary, that's all.

Cut pheasants in serving pieces, roll in seasoned flour, brown in melted butter in skillet which has a tight fitting lid. When the browning is nearly completed, add ¼ cup minced onion and sprinkle the birds with 1 tbsp. Hungarian paprika. (If you are unable to obtain the real McCoy, be as liberal as you wish with what we call pulverized brick). Add ½ cup stock or water, cover tightly and simmer until tender, adding more liquid if necessary. Remove birds to heated platter. Blend 2 tbsps. flour into pan juices, slowly add 1 cup game bird stock, stirring constantly until smooth and thickened. Add 1 cup sour cream, some grated lemon rind and 1 tbsp. lemon juice. Continue to heat until almost at the boiling point, pour a bit of sauce over pheasant and sprinkle with paprika. Serve balance of sauce in a preheated bowl —with noodles and cabbage.

WILD RICE CASSEROLE

1 stewing pheasant or 2 to 3 grouse of comparable age	½ lb. sautéed mushrooms
	½ onion, minced
⅔ cup wild rice	2 stalks celery, finely diced
Game bird stock (or chicken)	1 green pepper, diced

Cover disjointed birds with chicken or game bird stock and simmer until tender. Remove meat and cut in large dice. Boil wild rice in stock birds were cooked in until rice is half done—about 20 minutes. In buttered casserole, combine rice, fowl, vegetables, adding small amount of stock to finish cooking rice. Cover casserole and bake at 350° for ½ hour. Garnish casserole with pimento strips and parsley sprigs.

Quail

This little bird, beloved by sportsman and gourmet alike, is the one most often hunted and bagged in the United States. The range of the quail family extends from coast to coast, primarily in the southern regions. The best known, of course, is the Bobwhite, often called a partridge; others include the Desert, Massena, Mountain, Scaled and Valley. These delicate white fleshed morsels (only 5 to 6 oz. each) are best done in simple fashion with no potent seasonings to mask their delicious flavor.

SAUTEED QUAIL WITH MUSHROOMS

Rub with cut side of a lemon, season birds inside and out with salt and pepper. Brown quail along with sliced mushrooms in skillet in melted butter. Add ½ cup white wine when birds are nicely browned on all sides, toss in a few parsley sprigs, cover and simmer 10 to 15 minutes —until birds are tender. Dish each bird into a trencher, discard wilted parsley, pour over mushrooms and sauce and garnish with fresh parsley.

Note for the cook: If you're as tired as I am of searching for *really fresh* parsley in the markets, try growing your own. A packet of seed sown in early spring will give you parsley all summer long and its attractive foliage blends well with low border plants in your flower garden. In the fall, dig out several plants, pot them up and keep them on your kitchen window sill—Voila! parsley when you want it and a bright spot of green in your kitchen.

Trenchers for Quail and Other Small Birds

Take large rolls or small loaves of bread, just slightly larger than the birds you are using. Cut off the tops and scoop out the soft crumbs, leaving only a shell. Dry and grind the crumbs for other uses. Butter the bread shells liberally and toast in a slow oven until they are very crisp and lightly browned. This way they will retain their crunchiness even when they have absorbed the juices from the birds.

QUAIL WITH CHERRY SAUCE

This is another treasure from old Vienna, adaptable to other small birds.

In a flameproof casserole, brown the quail in butter on all sides, season lightly with salt and pepper, cover and place in oven preheated to 400° for 15 to 20 minutes. Place the birds on a heated platter and keep warm while you prepare the sauce in the casserole in which the birds were cooked. See Chap. X for Cherry sauce.

ROAST QUAIL WITH GRAPES

Season quail with salt and pepper, place a grape leaf on the breast of each bird, then wrap in bacon strips and tie. Roast in shallow pan in oven preheated to 450° for 15 to 20 minutes, basting frequently with melted butter. When quail are done, place on trenchers and keep warm. Add ¼ cup water to roasting pan, bring to boil, scraping pan. Lower heat, add 3 or 4 tbsps. dry sherry or white wine, ½ cup seedless green grapes and simmer several minutes. Just before serving, add a handful of chopped, toasted filberts if desired. (Filberts are not always available in our area, and since I use them quite often, I buy a good supply at holiday time and then keep them in the freezer.)

QUAIL ESTERHAZY

1 quail per serving	Onion, finely minced
1 hard roll, slightly larger than quail, per serving	Bay leaf, crushed
	White wine
Butter	Milk
Thyme and ground clove, if desired	Bacon slices
	Salt

Sprinkle quail inside and out with salt and pepper. With a sharp knife, cut each hard roll in half, gently pull out soft crumbs inside rolls. Make a stuffing of: roll crumbs, melted butter, onion gently sautéed in butter, thyme and bay leaf (plus a sprinkle of clove, if desired). Moisten with a bit of white wine and toss lightly to blend. Stuff the quail lightly, do not pack. Place each bird between two roll halves, moisten tops of the rolls with milk, and place a slice of bacon atop each roll. Tie or skewer together and place in a shallow pan.

Roast in a slow oven until tender—325° for about 35 to 40 minutes. Serve with red cabbage and boiled potatoes.

Wild Turkey

Wild turkey is truly the king of the game birds—not only in size but in the skill with which he eludes the most crafty hunter. The kingdom of this regal bird extended from New England and Canada to Mexico in the 14th and 15th centuries. As civilization marched across the continent, the domain of this bird of the forest has been diminished. Today the wild turkey is a rarity in the northern and central states— even in southern states where he is found in abundance, it takes a skilled hunter to bag this wary and alert bird. Male wild turkeys average 15 lbs. and are stuffed, trussed and cooked in the same manner as the domesticated birds. However, allowance must be made for their lack of fat.

ROAST WILD TURKEY

Prepare your favorite stuffing, allowing about 1 cup per pound of bird, dressed weight. Perhaps, since this is a rare treat, you might like to try something a bit special—browse through Chap. X and decide.

I would suggest cooking a larger (and therefore older) bird in foil. This method has several advantages: the most important in this case is that the meat does not have an opportunity to dry out, basting is almost completely eliminated and the steam within the foil helps tenderize even the hardiest old gobbler.

Here's how to proceed:

Cover entire stuffed and trussed bird with a liberal coating of softened shortening or butter. Pad wing tips, tail and leg ends with double folds of foil to prevent puncturing of the foil wrapper. Tear off sufficient foil of the heavy-duty variety to cover the entire bird loosely. You may have to use two pieces, double-folded together. Place the foil on a large shallow pan, set the bird in the center and bring the long ends of the foil over the breast of the bird, folding together loosely. Turn up the foil at each end in a single fold at least 4" from the outer edge of the foil. The wrapping should not be completely airtight, but should prevent the drippings from running out. Roast in a hot oven, preheated to 450°, according to the following table:

Oven-ready weight	Cooking time
8 lbs.	2½ hrs.
10 lbs.	2¾ hrs.
12 lbs.	3¼ hrs.
15 lbs.	3½ hrs.
20 lbs.	3¾ to 4 hrs.

About 45 minutes before you expect the bird to be done, carefully open the wrapper and fold the foil back in pan fashion. Check for tenderness of the thigh by pressing the meat—protect your hand with a paper towel. Return bird to oven to finish browning, basting frequently from this point on. When bird is done, remove pan juices with a basting syringe to a saucepan, lift bird to a heated platter and remove strings or skewers. Set the bird in a warming oven for 20 minutes while you prepare gravy.

Woodcock

Although the woodcock is included among the upland birds, he is actually a member of the snipe clan of shore birds. He has deserted the shore line habitat of his brethren and seems to prosper well near cultivated land. As a matter of fact, we have seen them not 50 ft. from our house, boring for worms and grubs in the soft earth beside the stream. It takes a bit of looking to see woodcock, since they are masters of camouflage and usually begin feeding only at twilight. Hunting the mysterious little birds is a sporty but strenuous affair and is becoming more popular every year.

Hunters who are successful in their quest of the woodcock have a rare treat in store, for the dark meat of these birds is considered the best of all game birds. The English consider the trail of the woodcock a great delicacy and do not draw the birds, but merely wipe them with a soft cloth. However, this is a matter of personal taste and I don't feel it necessary to follow this tradition—I prefer them cleaned in the same manner as any other game bird. Any of the recipes for quail may also be used for woodcock—allow one bird per serving.

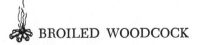 BROILED WOODCOCK

Season with salt and pepper, wrap in bacon or larding pork and broil over moderate coals for a total of 15 to 18 minutes. Arrange a drip pan of foil to catch the juices as the bird broils—it is generally cooked only to the pink stage and not well done. Serve with crisp croutons or toast, as with quail.

ROAST WOODCOCK

Season with salt and pepper, place the bird's liver and a piece of butter in the cavity. Roast in an oven preheated to 375°. After 10 minutes, baste with 1 tbsp. butter and ½ cup cream per bird. Continue roasting for another 15 minutes, basting at least once more. Serve on croutons with the sauce poured over. The livers may be mashed on the croutons or served inside the bird, as you wish.

Woodcock are also delicious roasted as above, but stuffed with a veal forcemeat (see Chap. X).

CASSEROLE OF WOODCOCK

For each bird to be served: Bacon slices
¼ cup raw diced chicken livers   2 tbsps. butter
½ cup Madeira   ¼ cup game bird stock
1 tsp. lemon juice   Salt and pepper

Stuff each bird with the diced livers which have been cooked for 5 minutes in ¼ cup Madeira and the lemon juice. Wrap each bird in bacon slices and brown in butter in a flameproof casserole. Add the stock and the balance of the Madeira and season to taste with salt and pepper. Cover casserole tightly and place in oven preheated to 400° —15 to 20 minutes is sufficient. Serve from the casserole, which has been garnished with croutons and fresh parsley.

Shore Birds

This classification includes the coot, gallinule, rail and snipe.

Coot

Although the coot is frequently found in the company of ducks, the coot, or marsh-hen, is a member of the rail family, and is found in shallow ponds and muddy bogs. Its diet is primarily vegetable, but occasionally you will find a fish-eater. Coot should be skinned as soon as possible after shooting. Prompt drawing and cleaning is a must. If you suspect that you have a few fish-eaters in your bag, then a marinade might be advisable in addition to the prompt cleaning and skinning.

MARINADE FOR COOT

1 cup water	1 bay leaf
1 cup wine vinegar or lemon juice	1 sliced onion
1 tsp. salt	1 sliced carrot
½ tsp. pepper	1 stalk celery, sliced

Combine all ingredients and boil for 5 minutes. Cool and marinate the coots for a few hours in a cool place.

SAUTEED COOT

Remove the breast meat in two filets and cut off the legs at the thigh joint. Marinate as directed above, then drain and saute in butter, season with salt and freshly ground pepper, cover and simmer for 20 minutes, or until tender. Remove the coot to a hot platter and blend ½ glass tart jelly and 1 tsp. lemon juice with the pan drippings. Pour over the birds and serve.

BRAISED COOT

Brown the coot breasts and legs in butter, season with salt and pepper, reduce flame and add equal amounts of stock and white wine to cover (or use a part of the marinade as liquid). Cover and simmer until tender. Thicken the gravy with roux (plus tart jelly, if desired) and serve.

Gallinule

The Florida and purple gallinules, like their English cousin the moorhen, can best be described as chickens who deserted the barnyard for the bogs and marshes. They do not rank among the highest as table food, but can be delicious when skinned and braised.

BRAISED GALLINULE

Brown the split birds in butter or drippings, season rather highly with salt and cayenne, cover and simmer slowly for ½ hour. Add Italian sauce (see Chap. X) and simmer for an additional ½ hour or until tender.

Snipe

Snipe, like woodcock, are considered a great delicacy. These little long-billed creatures are protected in many areas, but even where snipe shooting is legal, hunters will pass up the opportunity in favor of the larger birds. It's a pity, for the snipe not only provides good shooting, but also good eating. Any of the recipes given for woodcock are appropriate—however, the snipe is skinned before cooking.

 BROILED SNIPE

Season lightly with salt and pepper, wrap birds in bacon slices and skewer. Broil over moderate coals with a drip pan to catch the juices —about 15 minutes is sufficient. Meanwhile, chop the liver, heart and gizzard and cook gently in butter with parsley, nutmeg and salt. Make golden brown toast, spread the liver etc. on it, place the cooked birds on the toast and pour the pan drippings over all.

An alternate sauce may be made from the giblets in this way: cook the giblets as described above, then add ½ cup white wine and ½ cup sour cream. Blend in 1 tbsp. fine dry breadcrumbs and a small amount of grated lemon peel. Pour the sauce over the birds and garnish the platter with croutons.

SNIPE WITH SHERRY

Brown the snipe in butter, season with minced parsley, a bit of finely minced shallot or scallion, salt and pepper and a fresh grating of nutmeg. Add ¼ cup sherry per bird plus 1 tsp. lemon juice. Reduce heat, cover and simmer for 20 minutes. Serve on buttered toast or trenchers.

Rail

The confirmed rail hunter is truly a devoted one, especially in the tidal marshlands of New Jersey. The heat and the mosquitoes are fierce at the time of the rail migrations. If the rail shooter is successful, the plump little birds, which feed on wild rice, will provide a delectable meal. Unlike snipe, these birds are always plucked, never skinned. Recipes for quail and snipe may be used.

ROAST RAIL

Season with salt and pepper, stuff with veal forcemeat (see Chap. X) and wrap in bacon slices. Roast in oven preheated to 400° for 30 minutes, basting frequently with melted butter. Serve on toast or trenchers.

BREADED RAIL

Split the birds as you would a broiling chicken, season with salt and pepper, dip in beaten egg and then in fine dry crumbs which have been seasoned with a pinch of marjoram. Saute gently in butter, allowing 15 minutes per side. Serve with wedges of lemon.

RAIL CURRY

2 or 3 rail
½ cup minced onions
¼ cup butter
1 tbsp. curry powder
2 cups chicken or
    game bird stock
1 tbsp. flour

Salt and pepper to taste

Split the rail, brown in butter and set aside. In the same pan, brown the onion and curry powder, blend in the flour and then the stock, stirring until all is thickened and smooth. Add salt and pepper to taste, return the birds to the sauce, cover and simmer for ½ hour or until tender. Rice, chutney and the usual curry accompaniments should be provided.

Wild Ducks

Among those most desirable for the table are the mallard, black, widgeon, canvasback, pintail, redhead, ring-necked and teal. For the most part, these birds are vegetarians and their dark flesh is considered a delicacy the world over. However, each duck is only as good as its diet and some of the vegetarians do resort occasionally to a diet of fish and crustaceans. Prompt drawing and cleaning of ducks will eliminate the possibility of the "fishy" taste to a great extent.

Ducks should be dry plucked and not skinned. To remove the down which remains, *don't* plunge them into hot water in which paraffin has been melted. If the water is hot enough to melt the paraffin, it's hot enough to parboil the skin of the duck. Instead, melt paraffin in the top part of a double boiler over hot water (never over a direct flame) and allow the wax to cool slightly. Paint the wax on the ducks and let it harden, then zip off wax and down together.

Most purists insist that ducks not be washed, but merely wiped clean with a soft cloth. On the other extreme, there are those who advocate soaking for hours in buttermilk or salt water. A quick rinse in cold water as part of the cleaning process is not detrimental, especially if the flesh has been badly damaged by shot—just be sure to dry the duck thoroughly afterwards. A piece of celery or onion in the duck cavity while it is aging in the refrigerator is the accepted method of eliminating the last vestiges of strong flavor. This "stuffing" is discarded before cooking.

In contrast to domestic ducks, wild ducks need larding or basting to prevent the flesh from drying out, especially under intense heat. Most people prefer wild duck at least slightly rare—this requires only a *total* of 18 to 25 minutes in a 450° to 475° oven. If you like duck well done, then use one of the recipes where moist heat is used. Do not attempt to roast or broil ducks to the well done stage—they are very apt to be tough and dry.

CANARD A L'ORANGE

Preheat oven to 450°. Stuff ducks with apricot-rice stuffing (see Chap. X) and truss. Combine ½ cup orange juice and 2 tbsps. butter for basting sauce. Roast ducks for ½ hour, basting frequently. Prepare gravy by boiling up pan juices, stirring to loosen any browned particles, add a bit more orange juice if necessary. Thicken slightly with a bit of roux blended in and add several tbsps. tart orange marmalade.

Garnish the platter with glazed orange slices and watercress. (see Chap. IX for glazed orange slices)

ROAST DUCK WITH SAVORY WILD RICE

Stuff ducks with savory wild rice (see Chap. X), season with salt and pepper, lard with bacon slices and roast at 450° 25 minutes, basting frequently with port wine and butter. Several spoons of red currant jelly may be melted in the pan juices for gravy.

ROAST DUCK WITH SAUERKRAUT

Insert a piece of apple and half a small onion in the cavity of each duck, along with a juniper berry, if desired. Season ducks with salt and pepper and lard with bacon slices. Set ducks aside while you prepare the sauerkraut and preheat the oven to 425°. Combine and brown in saucepan 2 tbsps. butter and 2 diced bacon slices. Add 3 cups sauerkraut and 1½ tsps. caraway seed. Blend well and simmer 20 minutes. Place the sauerkraut in roaster, set the ducks on top and roast 18 to 25 minutes, depending on size of the ducks. Baste with melted butter at least once during roasting.

SALMI OF DUCK IN RED WINE

Brace of older ducks,
   cut in serving pieces
Butter
2 cups red wine
¼ cup brandy
1 onion, sliced
2 carrots, sliced
2 stalks celery, sliced

4 sprigs parsley
1 tsp. salt
½ tsp. pepper
   Pinch of thyme and marjoram
½ lb. mushrooms,
   sautéed in butter

Marinate the duck in a glass bowl with all ingredients listed except the butter and mushrooms. After 2 or 3 hours, drain the duck and brown in hot butter in flameproof casserole. Add the marinade, including the sliced vegetables, and simmer over a low flame until tender—about 1 hour. Remove the duck pieces to a hot platter, strain the marinade into a saucepan, thicken with roux, stir until smooth, and add mushrooms. Serve with wild rice.

BROILED DUCK—*Cantonese*

Basting sauce:

¼ cup honey   ¼ cup sherry
    Small clove of garlic, crushed   ½ tsp. ginger
3 tbsps. soy sauce   Pinch of dry mustard

Combine the above ingredients. Season the cavities of young ducks
with salt and pepper, place a piece of celery and a slice of lemon in
each cavity. Balance and truss on a spit. Broil over moderate coals,
turning and basting frequently with sauce, for approximately 20 minutes. Serve with white rice.

BRAISED DUCKLING

Cut a brace of ducks into serving pieces, brown in melted butter in
dutch oven, season with salt and pepper. Add 1 cup orange juice, 1
cup chicken broth, ⅔ cup golden raisins. Cover and simmer gently
until tender. Remove birds, blend in ½ cup tart jelly and thicken if
necessary with a bit of roux. Pour the sauce over the birds and serve
with rice.

Since orange and grapefruit crystals are now available for camp-
ers, this dish can be prepared easily at camp. Just add water in
the proportions directed, dissolve a bouillon cube in water for the
broth, and there you are. Raisins should be no problem—if you don't
already include them in your camp kit for quick energy, do so next
time. Our hunting jacket pockets always have a few small packages
tucked into them.

DUCK IN CREOLE SAUCE

Brown duck, cut in serving pieces, in dutch oven in melted butter.
Add Creole sauce (see Chap. X) to cover and simmer until tender.
Serve with rice.

BOHEMIAN DUCK WITH TURNIP

Brace of ducks   ¼ cup butter
    (older birds would be fine)   Salt and pepper

½ cup white wine   Paprika
3 cups peeled diced yellow turnip   ½ cup sour cream

In flameproof casserole, cook turnip covered with 2 tbsps. butter, salt and pepper, paprika and wine for 15 minutes. Season and brown ducks in butter, place birds atop turnips, pour over the butter in which the ducks were browned. Cover the casserole and simmer until the ducks are tender. Remove ducks to heated platter, drain off any excess liquid in the casserole, blend the sour cream with the turnip and then arrange around the birds. Sprinkle with paprika and serve.

CLAY BIRD

This one is fun to do and the results are delicious—I have done it myself, so I offer it here with the necessary warnings. *IF* you have time while preparing breakfast, packing lunch, getting decoys and sneak box ready to go at 3:00 A.M., blessings on you! If one of your hunting buddies elects to stay in camp and loaf one day, this is a good one to remember.

Find yourself some good sticky clay—nothing else will do, so if that's not available, forget it till next time. Dig a pit and build a good fire that will burn down to lasting coals. Stuff a cleaned but unplucked duck with apple and/or onion and piece of celery, fasten the openings closed and fold the feathers over to keep out the clay. Then plaster the bird liberally with clay—the sticky overcoat should be at least an inch thick, if not more. Scrape aside some of the coals, set the bird in the coals and pile others on top. Seal the pit and forget about it till you're ready to eat. Dig the bird out carefully, knock off the hardened clay (the feathers will come too) and start eating!

Wild Geese

It is hard to say whether goose or turkey shooting ranks higher among gunners. Both goose and turkey are a challenge to the hunter's skill, both are splendid for the table. The geese most often found in the United States include the blue, brant, Canada, white-fronted and snow, both greater and lesser. The lesser snow goose is preferred for table use, as its diet makes the flesh more palatable than that of the greater snow goose.

Depending on the species, geese average between 5 and 9 lbs. Older birds, more suitably cooked by moist heat methods, are identified by coarse plumage and very large wingspurs. The young geese are most delicious roasted with a tart fruit stuffing to enhance the succulence of their dark meat.

BRAISED GOOSE

Stuff an older goose with sage and celery bread dressing. Place in dutch oven or roaster with a tight-fitting lid, along with ½ cup of each of the following: chopped carrot, chopped celery, onion and ham. Add 1 cup stock and 1 or 2 juniper berries. Braise in hot oven, covered, at 425° for 1½ hours or until tender. Meanwhile, reduce over a slow fire 1 cup game bird stock until it has reached the jelly stage. Remove the goose to a heated platter, brush with the glaze and keep hot. Strain the juices from the dutch oven into a saucepan, thicken with roux, bring to a boil, stirring constantly. Add ½ glass white wine and simmer for another minute. Pour into preheated sauce boat. Serve with glazed apple rings or raw cranberry relish in orange cups. (see Chap. IX)

BRAISED GOOSE WITH APPLES

Stuff an older goose with celery and onion slices. Season with salt and pepper and place in covered roaster. Peel and core several large tart cooking apples, cut into thick slices and place around the goose. Roast covered at 425° for 20 to 25 minutes per lb., basting frequently with cider. Uncover the roaster the last few minutes to allow the goose to brown. Remove onion and celery before serving.

JUGGED GOOSE

Clean an older goose and cook as directed under game bird stock (see Chap. II). Simmer until tender, remove the goose from the broth and cool. Cut with poultry shears into serving portions. Beat 1 egg with 1 tbsp. dry white wine, dip each piece of goose into egg, then into seasoned fine dry bread-crumbs. Sauté gently in butter until golden brown. Serve with any of the following sauces: Madeira sauce, Apricot game sauce, or white wine sauce (see Chap. X). If you prepare white wine sauce, boil up 2 cups of the stock in which the goose was cooked until it is reduced by half.

ROAST YOUNG GOOSE

Clean a young goose and stuff with any preferred stuffing. You might try one of the following: cranberry, chestnut, apricot, prune and apple (see Chap. X). Season the outside of the goose with salt and pepper and a light dash of ginger or cloves (whichever complements the stuffing best). Roast at 325° for 18 to 20 minutes per lb., basting frequently. The basting liquid should be made up of melted butter plus one of the following: apple juice, cider, orange juice, red or white wine. Select the flavor which will blend best with the stuffing. When the goose is tender, the thigh joint will move easily. Since roast goose is a festive dish, you may wish to add another special touch at this point, by glazing the goose. Combine 2 tbsps. of basting liquid with ½ cup clear tart jelly and brush over the bird. Return to the oven for 15 minutes. Prepare gravy from the pan juices, plus stock or the liquid in which the giblets were cooked. Garnish appropriately, according to the stuffing used.

CHAPTER VI

Small Game

SMALL GAME, often found right in your own back yard or pretty close to it, can be equally as delicious as the prime roasts from the deer or elk you travelled so far to bag.

Not 10 minutes' drive from here are beaver and muskrat, and right in our back yard we have rabbits, chucks, opossum, racoon and squirrel. Unfortunately, we are just within the village limits, so I can't take a poke at them from the doorstep. Not that I haven't been tempted —especially by the rabbits which have gorged themselves on my young vegetable and flower plants, and by the squirrels which constantly rob my bird feeders.

Beaver

As Mrs. Dalziel says in her recipe for beaver tail (see Chap. XI), "First you must get acquainted with a beaver hunter", to which I must add "or trapper", for in most areas these animals are trapped for their valuable pelts. There is a lot of good eating on a beaver; a mature animal will weigh up to 50 or 60 lbs. However, if you are offered a choice by your trapper friend, take a younger animal, for the meat will be more tender. Young beaver, with its dark rich meat, is delicious roasted. The older ones will make a good pot roast or stew.

ROAST YOUNG BEAVER

Strip all possible fat from the beaver. Preheat oven to 450°, season with salt and pepper and place on a rack in the roaster. Cook at this high heat for 15 to 20 minutes to sear the outside, then lower the heat to 325° to 350° and roast for 30 minutes per lb. Slice an onion over the top of the roast if you wish. In contrast to the big game animals, this critter needs no basting—the rack is advisable so that the fat still within the beaver will not collect around the roast itself.

CHICKEN FRIED BEAVER

Cut a young beaver into serving portions. Parboil in salted water with an onion, if desired, until the beaver is nearly tender. This parboiling helps to remove any excess fat. Drain the beaver pieces and roll in crumbs or flour seasoned with salt, pepper, thyme or sage, and then brown slowly in a heavy skillet in butter or drippings. Make gravy by blending into the pan drippings any of the dehydrated soup mixes with an appropriate amount of water.

 **BEAVER STEW**

3 lbs. boned beaver, cut in cubes
  Drippings
  Flour
  Salt and pepper
  Bay leaf
  Dash of Worcestershire sauce
  Water to cover
  Carrots

  Potatoes
  Onions
  Turnips and cabbage
    if available

Strip all possible fat from the beaver meat, flour the cubes and brown on all sides in small amount of fat in the dutch oven. Season with salt and pepper, add water to cover, bay leaf and Worcestershire sauce. Cover and simmer until tender—the time will vary, naturally. When the meat is nearly tender, add the diced potatoes, carrots, onions and whatever else is available. Cover and simmer until the vegetables are tender but still recognizable. Thicken the gravy, if needed, with flour and water paste.

Muskrat

Muskrat is another dark meated bonus from the trapper. I see no reason not to call a spade a spade or a muskrat by its own name—so forget about the "Marsh-rabbit", "Swamp-rabbit", or "Marsh-hare". If your lady-fair has accepted and done well by other game you've brought home, she'll accept this one too—and on its own merits. Just be sure, before you present it for her fond attention in the kitchen, that you've removed all the small kernels or glands which could impair the otherwise delicious flavor.

ROAST MUSKRAT

Season inside and out with salt and pepper. Stuff with a savory bread and onion dressing or a prune and apple stuffing (see Chap. X). Sew or skewer openings, lard with bacon slices or brush liberally with butter. Roast on a rack in a moderate oven (350°), basting frequently with the pan drippings and a bit of hot water. When the muskrat is tender, remove the bacon slices and allow the meat to brown attractively the last 15 minutes.

If you suspect the muskrat is not too young, one of the following recipes will produce equally good results.

MUSKRAT IN CREOLE SAUCE

Cut muskrat in serving pieces, brown well in oil or butter in skillet which has a tight-fitting lid. Add Creole sauce to cover and simmer until very tender. Use a very low flame and check occasionally to be sure the sauce is not sticking to the pan. Serve with fluffy rice. (see Chap. X for Creole sauce)

BRAISED MUSKRAT

Cut muskrat in serving pieces, roll in seasoned flour and brown in dutch oven along with 2 sliced onions. Use butter or drippings. When all is evenly browned, reduce heat and add either 1 cup sour cream or 1 can of cream of mushroom soup. Cover tightly and simmer until tender.

Opossum

Although I have seen 'possum here and near our former home in the East, I would not have cooked them in either case. 'Possum will eat anything and those found near civilization are apt to be carrion and garbage eaters. Their meat can be unappetizing under such circumstances. However, friends from the South tell me that they are superb when they have been feeding on persimmons and berries. Because of the glands in the small of the back and inside the forelegs, it is preferred to skin these animals and remove the glands at that time. Age for a few days in the refrigerator as directed in Chap. I and be certain all excess fat is stripped off.

ROAST 'POSSUM

There are two ways to proceed with his favorite dish of the Old South. Both are designed to rid the 'possum of excess fat.

Parboil in salted water to cover for about 1 hour. Then place in a roaster in a 350° oven, draining off fat as it accumulates. After the roast has browned a bit, season with salt and pepper and a sprinkle of sage or poultry seasoning. After an hour of roasting, add sweet potatoes which have been parboiled 20 minutes in their jackets and then skinned and cut in thick slices. Sprinkle the sweet potato slices with brown sugar and add a dot of butter to each slice, if you wish. Continue roasting until 'possum and potatoes are tender—about ½ hour.

Preheat oven to 450°, place the 'possum on a rack in the roaster and roast at high heat for 15 to 20 minutes. Reduce the oven heat to 350°, season with salt and pepper and roast uncovered for about an hour, draining off fat as it accumulates. Place scrubbed sweet potatoes in their jackets in the roaster and continue baking till both are tender.

CAMPFIRE 'POSSUM

Cut a young 'possum in serving pieces, and broil over the coals of your campfire, turning frequently so the pieces are nicely browned. Serve with sweet potatoes which have been roasting in their jackets in the embers of the fire.

Porcupine

The porcupine is protected by law and/or tradition in most places to provide food for the lost and hungry. The slow-moving porky does not attack or "shoot" its quills, as so many believe. The porcupine can be done in with a rock or a club, but even when he is dead, his quills can do damage. If you're that hungry, do as the Indians did—just throw the porky on the coals of a fire, heap with more coals and roast for about an hour. Then remove the burned hide and eat the flesh.

However, if you're not in such a tearing hurry, it is better to skin the porky, in order to remove the excess fat. Approach the skinning job from the smooth underneath part of the beast and you should have no trouble.

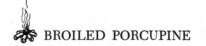

BROILED PORCUPINE

Since porky fat has the same tallowy consistency as lamb or mutton, it is best to cook the meat over the coals of an open fire. If a small young one, spit the entire beast—a larger one can be cut in pieces and broiled in the same manner. Done in this way, the excess fat will drip out into the fire and the remainder can then be eaten cold as you go on your way.

PORCUPINE STEW

If you have an older porcupine, you may have up to 40 lbs. of meat, and that should be enough to sustain you for some time. Parboil the meat in salted water to remove the excess fat and to help tenderize the meat. Finish the cooking over the open fire or make a stew if you happen to have any other supplies with you. As I have said before, hunger is the best seasoning and in an emergency, whatever you can devise is just dandy.

Rabbit and Hare

Rabbits and hares are still the most abundant and popular game animals in the United States. As a matter of fact, these furry vegetarians are favorites all over the world. The meat is mild in flavor, very similar to chicken, and can be prepared in the same way as chicken. The best indication of age, and therefore of your cooking method, is the ear. If the ear is soft and splits easily, the rabbit or hare is young and may be fried or roasted. A tough ear means a critter for the stew pot or dutch oven. I mentioned it before, but it bears repeating—rabbit should always be well done to avoid any possible infection from tularemia.

PAN-FRIED RABBIT

Cut young rabbits in serving pieces, dip in egg which has been beaten with 1 tbsp. water, then roll in flour or fine crumbs which have been seasoned with salt, pepper and a pinch of thyme. Heat butter in a heavy skillet and brown the rabbit over low heat until golden brown. Cover and let the skillet sit at the edge of your fire until the rabbit is well done. A sprinkle of lemon juice, if available, is a welcome addition when serving.

BROILED RABBIT

Split young rabbits in half, season with salt and pepper, wrap in bacon slices or baste liberally with butter while broiling slowly over moderate coals. A judicious slit with your knife near the bone will indicate whether or not the meat is well done.

ROAST RABBIT

Stuff young rabbits with a celery and onion bread dressing, skewer or sew up openings. Season outside with salt and pepper and dust lightly with flour. Cover the rabbits with bacon slices and place in roaster with enough stock or chicken broth to cover the bottom of the roaster. Cover the roaster and place in 350° oven for 1 to 1½ hours, basting several times with the pan juices. When the rabbits are tender, remove the bacon slices and return the roaster to the oven uncovered, so that the rabbits can brown for a few minutes. Remove the rabbits to a heated platter and prepare gravy from the pan juices, a bit of roux and stock or cream.

RABBIT IN ASPIC—*Viennese Style*

This recipe was translated from a very old Viennese cook book. It's strictly party fare, but well worth the effort. It would be most attractive served as an appetizer or for a cold buffet.

> 1 whole saddle of young hare or plump rabbit
> Larding pork, cut in long thin strips
> Clear aspic

Remove the entire saddle from a cleaned rabbit or hare and set aside while you prepare the aspic. Disjoint the remainder of the rabbit and place in a covered kettle. Add water to cover, 1 tbsp. salt per quart of water, 1 carrot, 1 stalk celery including the leaves, 1 medium onion, a pinch of thyme and a few peppercorns. Cover and simmer over low heat. When the rabbit is tender, remove from the bones and reserve for future use. If stock is not strong enough at this point, return the bones to the kettle and reduce by boiling—or you may add 1 or 2 chicken bouillon cubes. Strain and clarify as directed in Chap. II. There should be at least 3½ cups clarified stock.

Soften 2 tbsps. unflavored gelatin in ½ cup cold stock, then dissolve completely in 1 cup hot stock. Add a liberal pinch of saffron and 1 tbsp. lemon juice, then stir until the saffron has released all its color to the liquid. Pour through a fine sieve to remove saffron particles and combine with the remaining stock. Select a flat platter long enough to hold the saddle, rinse the platter in cold water and spoon a layer of aspic onto the platter and chill. Set the remaining aspic aside where it will not set.

Lard the saddle liberally with strips of pork fat in an attractive pattern, drawing the strips through the length of the saddle with a larding needle. Place in baking pan, tent with greaseproof paper or aluminum foil and roast at 350° to 375°, basting frequently until tender but still juicy. This will take about an hour, but be sure that the larding pork is still visible and has not all cooked out. Remove from the oven and cool. When saddle is cold, remove the filets from the ribs carefully with a thin sharp knife. Place the two filets on the layer of aspic in such a way that the saddle appears to be whole. Spoon over it the remainder of the aspic which should by now have the consistency of unbeaten egg white. Set in the refrigerator to jell completely. It must appear as if the meat is covered with thick yellow glass. Garnish with watercress, freshly grated horseradish and red radishes.

HASENPFEFFER

1 large rabbit or hare   Drippings
   or 2 smaller ones
    cut into serving pieces
  Seasoned flour
¼ cup sour cream
1 tbsp. flour

Marinade consisting of:
  Equal parts of wine vinegar and
    water to cover rabbit
4 tsps. sugar to each
  cup of liquid
½ tsp. salt per cup of liquid
Few peppercorns
2 sliced onions
2 stalks celery or
  sliced celery knob

2 sliced carrots
2 or 3 juniper berries
Bay leaf
2 or 3 whole cloves

Combine the ingredients for the marinade in a glass bowl and add the rabbit pieces. Cover and marinate for 2 days in a cool place, turning the rabbit pieces twice daily. Drain and dry the rabbit, reserving the marinade. Coat the rabbit pieces with seasoned flour and brown in dutch oven in drippings. Reduce heat, add marinade and vegetables, cover and simmer until tender. Remove rabbit to heated platter and keep warm. Strain the sauce through a sieve, pressing the vegetables through also. Blend flour with sour cream and add slowly to the strained sauce, heating just to the boiling point. Serve with dumplings. (see Chap. XII)

RABBIT FRICASSEE

1 older rabbit or hare,
  cut in serving pieces
Butter or drippings
Flour
Salt and pepper
Bay leaf
Sprigs of parsley
Pinch of thyme
Celery, chopped

Carrot, chopped
Water or stock to cover

Coat rabbit pieces in seasoned flour, brown in hot butter in dutch oven, add stock or water to cover, vegetables and herbs. Cover dutch oven and set over a slow fire to simmer until rabbit is tender. Thicken gravy if necessary. If you want dumplings, add them to the bubbling liquid, cover tightly and steam for 20 minutes more—don't lift the lid! Place rabbit and dumplings on a hot platter and strain the gravy into a heated sauce boat. (see Chap. XII for dumplings)

CIVET DE LIEVRE

1 hare or large rabbit,
   cut in serving pieces
½ lb. bacon or
   salt pork, diced
Rabbit liver, firm and
   dark with no spots
2 onions, coarsely chopped
Flour

Salt and pepper
Dry red wine to cover or equal
   amounts of wine and stock
Bouquet garni: thyme, bay leaf,
   parsley, small garlic clove
½ lb. fresh mushrooms
4 tbsps. butter
18 to 20 small white onions

Season rabbit pieces with salt and pepper and coat with flour. In a covered skillet or dutch oven, brown bacon lightly—then remove bacon pieces. Brown rabbit on all sides in the same fat, adding the chopped onion during the last of the browning process so it does not scorch. Add wine (and stock) to cover the rabbit, bouquet garni and bacon pieces. Cover and simmer over low flame until tender (about 2 hours). In another skillet, sauté mushrooms in butter for 5 minutes, add rabbit liver, chopped and sauté another 2 to 3 minutes. Add liver and mushrooms to rabbit in dutch oven, along with onions which have been parboiled in salted water for 15 minutes and then drained. Combine and heat thoroughly. Remove the bouquet garni and place rabbit and vegetables on warm serving platter. Thicken gravy with flour and water paste, stir until boiling and let the gravy simmer for 2 or 3 minutes. Pour over rabbit and serve.

RABBIT IN WHITE WINE SAUCE

1 large rabbit or hare
   or 2 small ones
Larding pork or bacon slices
2 or 3 tbsps. butter
1 onion, thinly sliced
1 carrot, thinly sliced
2 stalks celery, finely diced
1 parsnip or parsley root, diced
Salt and pepper
2 or 3 allspice berries

Pinch of thyme or marjoram
Rabbit stock
2 tbsps. vinegar
1 glass dry white wine
1 tbsp. lemon juice
Grated lemon rind
1 tsp. capers
2 tbsp. tomato paste
¼ cup sour cream

Cut away the forelegs, breast and belly flesh of the rabbit, retaining only the saddle and hindlegs for the roast. Cover the forelegs, etc.

with salted water and simmer to make stock for the casserole. In a covered flameproof casserole, melt butter, saute vegetables lightly. Place rabbits and seasonings on top of vegetables, add vinegar, wine and enough stock to cover the bottom of the casserole ½" deep. Cover and simmer until rabbit is tender, adding more stock only if necessary to prevent sticking. Remove meat to warming oven. Dust vegetables lightly with flour, stir until flour is blended, add a ladle of rabbit stock, lemon juice and rind, capers, tomato paste and sour cream. Stir until thoroughly blended and thickened. Put the sauce through a sieve, forcing the vegetables through also. Cut the rabbits in serving pieces, place on platter with Speckknödel (bacon dumplings—see Chap. XII). Pour sauce over all.

Forelegs, breast and any leftovers can be used to make a pate—see Chap. VIII.

Raccoon

There must be something to this 'coon hunting, where grown men go out at night and pursue Mr. Ringtail with hounds. Personally, I've never been able to get excited about chasing cross country, stumbling over stones, through brush and swamp—when it's so dark you can't see your hand in front of your face. But I do get a thrill out of listening to a pack of hounds as they pick up the scent, begin trailing and finally end in an orgy of barking "treed."

Old "rackety-coon" is perfectly adjusted to living a lonely existence in the wilds, but he also likes to live near people, sometimes waking them in the early dawn by knocking over the trash cans. If you hear a weird sound in the night—like a baby being tortured—friend 'coon is on the prowl. Not so amusing is the fact that Mr. Ringtail is a fierce fighter when backed into a corner by the hounds. More than one 'coon hound has lost his life when the 'coon enticed him into the water and then turned to the attack.

'Coon hunting is a matter of taste, but one fact you can't deny is that 'coon, properly prepared in the roaster, may be more to your taste than chasing him—I know I like it better!

ROOST 'COON

Parboil the 'coon in salted water to cover, adding carrots, onion and celery if you desire, for 30 to 60 minutes—depending on the size and age of the 'coon. As with 'possum, this helps remove some of the excess fat in the tissues. Drain and dry, then stuff with apple-raisin stuffing (see Chap. X), skewer and place on a rack in the roaster, adding a bit of apple juice to the bottom of the roaster. Roast at 350° for 40 to 45 minutes per lb. If the 'coon is a wily oldster, you may wish to cover the roast for a part of the cooking time, but be sure to uncover it the last ½ hour or so to allow him to brown nicely.

Any tart fruit stuffing goes well with Mr. Ringtail, as the flavor of the meat is very similar to the dark meat of chicken.

BROILED 'COON

If you've found yourself a youngster, broil him over a good bed of coals. Cut the meat in cubes, season well and thread on green sticks or skewers. Broil slowly until well browned and crisp on the outside. Have some apples and onions baking in the coals in foil packages nearby.

'COON STEW

4 lb. 'coon, cut in cubes	2 to 3 cups canned tomatoes
2 or 3 onions, sliced	Carrots
Salt and pepper	Onions
Bay leaf	Potatoes
Dash of Worcestershire sauce	Turnips

Brown the meat cubes slowly in a dutch oven—there should be enough fat within the tissues that no additional fat is required. Add the onions during the last of the browning process so they won't become scorched. Reduce the heat, add enough tomatoes and liquid to cover the meat, season and cover. Simmer on low flame until almost completely tender, then add cubed vegetables of your choice and continue to simmer until vegetables are tender. Check seasoning— you may want more salt—and serve with hot biscuits.

Squirrel

Beloved target of small and not-so-small boys, the squirrel ranks second only to the rabbit in popularity. The squirrel was an important item in the diet of the early settlers and is still a welcome addition to the game bag. The delicately flavored meat needs fat—either bacon or butter—in cooking and can be broiled, baked or stewed in the same manner as rabbit (see recipes on the preceding pages).

The most famous dish for squirrel is Brunswick Stew—a most delectable concoction to which I was introduced in Williamsburg, Va., while we were on our honeymoon. Nothing would do but for me to duplicate the recipe at home, as soon as we had obtained the necessary ingredients. I was still accustomed to helping cook for a large family, so I did not question the amounts in the recipe which had been given me. The two of us ate Brunswick Stew for almost a full week! P.S. I still use the same recipe, sometimes doubling it if there's a large crowd to feed. It freezes successfully and is a handy item for the "emergency" corner of my freezer.

BRUNSWICK STEW

The original recipe calls for squirrel only, but a combination of any or all of the following may be used with equally delicious results: squirrel, rabbit, woodchuck, pheasant—even chicken!

4 or 5 lbs. small game, disjointed
Diced bacon
3 sliced onions
Salt and pepper to taste
Water or stock to cover
2 quarts of tomatoes, drained
¼ to ½ tsp. cayenne pepper
Liberal sprinkling of thyme

3 or 4 potatoes, peeled and diced
2 cups fresh lima beans or the
   equivalent in frozen ones
2 cups fresh corn or the
   equivalent in frozen corn
2 cups okra, if available fresh
   —I find the frozen not too
   satisfactory in this dish

Brown the meat and onions in hot bacon fat in a dutch oven. Season with salt and pepper, add water or stock to cover the meat and simmer until tender. Remove the meat from the bones, return to the liquid and add potatoes, tomatoes, cayenne and thyme. Cook slowly for ½ hour, then add the fresh limas, corn and okra and cook until all is tender. (If frozen vegetables are used, they will require less time than the fresh ones.) Adjust seasonings before serving. Brunswick stew is usually served in soup plates, since it has the consistency of a thick soup. However, if you prefer, you may thicken it further with the addition of a bit of roux or some fine dry breadcrumbs. Corn pone or any corn bread is the traditional accompaniment. (see Chap. XII)

Woodchuck

Woodchuck, as well as their cousins the prairie dogs, have long been favored targets of the varmint shooters. Unfortunately, they have been neglected to a great extent in the culinary department. Young 'chucks, plump after a summer's gorging on grain and greens, are delicious roasted or broiled in the same fashion as 'coon, allowing of course for the difference in size. Just don't forget to strip off the fat and remove the gland kernels. If your 'chuck is a senior citizen, parboil him for half an hour in salted water and proceed as in Rabbit Fricassee —or set him aside in the freezer to add to that next Brunswick stew!

CHAPTER VII

Variety Meats

It has been a surprise to me to discover how many hunters discard —or ignore completely—the heart, liver, kidney, and tongue of the big game animals. You will seldom find a hunter of the old school who does not celebrate the conclusion of a successful hunt with one of these. One great advantage to these meats, in addition to their high nutritional value, is the fact that they can be prepared the same day the critter is shot. As a matter of fact, they are at their very best when fresh.

These organs or variety meats also keep well in the freezer for 3 to 4 months and are so delicious that they should never be wasted.

Liver

Although it is the organ most often saved, it is also the most often misunderstood. Just because the liver comes from an old, and perhaps tough, critter, it does not mean that it will require the same long slow cooking that the meat will. Liver is not muscular tissue and the only thing that makes it tough and hard is overcooking.

LIVER—*Celebration Supper*

The liver has already been rinsed with water and drained during the field dressing. Remove it from the plastic bag, give it another quick rinse in cold water and cut the liver in slices. We prefer liver still pink on the inside, so we cut slices at least ½" thick. If someone in your party is of the "well done" school, then cut his slices thinner than that. Remove the membrane covering on the edges of the slices by inserting the tip of your knife under the membrane and then pulling it away from the liver. Have everything else ready to eat and your diners assembled before liver ever touches frying pan. Use butter or bacon fat, whichever you prefer, flour the liver if you wish, but leave the salt and pepper on the table—it has no place here until the liver is cooked! Now into the pan—sear quickly on one side, turn and repeat on the other side—and that's it! The only exception I will make as far as rare liver is concerned is with bear, because of the possibility of trichinosis, and with rabbit, because of the danger of tularemia.

HIRSCHLEBER

This is the way the Central European hunters would do it. Remove outer membrane, slice liver. In butter or drippings, simmer sliced onions until golden brown, add liver slices and sauté only until no longer bloody. Remove liver to hot serving plate, to the hot drippings in the pan add salt and pepper, a sprinkle of garlic powder and ¼ cup vinegar. Bring to a boil quickly, stirring to loosen all crusty particles in the pan. Pour over liver and serve piping hot.

STUFFED DEER LIVER

This is a marvelous recipe for a fairly small liver, as the whole liver should be consumed at one sitting—one taste and you won't have any problems selling second helpings.

1 whole deer liver   ¼ cup bacon
  Bacon slices   ¼ cup anchovies
  Mixture of the following,
      finely chopped:
¼ cup onion

Remove outer membrane covering and tubes running through the liver. Place on a piece of cheesecloth large enough to enclose the entire liver. Cut deep gashes crosswise on the liver, but don't cut all the way through. In the first gash, place a whole strip of bacon; in the next gash, the mixture of chopped onion, bacon and anchovies—continue to stuff the gashes, alternating bacon slices and mixture. Tie the liver securely in the cheesecloth, sear on both sides in butter in a heavy skillet. Cover and cook *only* until liver is no longer bloody. Do not overcook, as this toughens it. Remove cheesecloth and slice at right angle to the gashes, so each slice has portions of the two stuffings. Serve with parsley potato balls.

LIVER LOAF

This is first cousin to the many fine pâtés—suitable for those who like their liver well done.

2 lbs. liver	½ green pepper, diced
6 to 8 slices of bacon	2 cups mashed potatoes
1 tsp. anchovy paste	3 eggs
1 onion, diced	Salt and pepper to taste

Cover liver with boiling water, let it stand 10 minutes. Drain thoroughly, then put liver and bacon through the fine blade of the food chopper. Beat eggs, add rest of the ingredients and blend thoroughly. Season to taste. Butter a loaf pan liberally, pack in the mixture and bake at 300° for 1½ hours. Serve cold with a sauce made of the following:

1 cup mayonnaise	Salt
4 to 5 tbsps. tomato puree	Cayenne pepper
1 tbsp. capers	

OR: bake the liver mixture in a greased ring mold and serve hot, with the center of the mold filled with creamed spinach.

BAKED LIVER SLICES

Slice liver thinly, allowing two slices per serving. Spread each slice with mushroom or sage bread stuffing. Roll and tie or skewer together. Place in buttered casserole, add ¾ cup game stock or beef bouillon and cover. Bake at 350° for 30 to 40 minutes, basting once or twice with the pan juices.

PATE   see Chap. XI

LEBERKNÖDEL (LIVER DUMPLINGS FOR SOUP)   see Chap. IX

HASENLEBER—*Rabbit Liver*

Be sure liver is firm and free from spots which indicate the presence of tularemia. Do not wash the livers, but soak in sweet milk for 24 hours. For each large rabbit or hare liver (or 2 small ones), melt 2 tbsps. butter and in it simmer ½ onion, minced, and 3 or 4 sprigs of parsley, chopped. Put in the coarsely chopped livers and simmer briskly for 10 minutes. When livers are done, put in for each liver 2 tbsps. sour cream and salt and pepper to taste. Let it simmer for 1 more minute, stirring constantly. Serve with French-fried potatoes and green salad.

WILD RICE WITH PHEASANT LIVERS

When we did a great deal of bird shooting in the East, I used to save the pheasant livers in the freezer until I had enough for this dish.

3 sliced onions
½ lb. butter
1 dozen pheasant livers,
    coarsely chopped

Salt and pepper to taste
2 cups wild rice, rinsed twice
    in boiling water
1 quart game bird stock
    or chicken bouillon

Sauté onions in butter in flameproof casserole until golden. Add pheasant livers, salt and pepper to taste and continue to stir over medium flame until browned. Add rice and stock and stir until water is bubbling again. Cover and place in 350° oven until rice is tender (about 40 minutes). At the end of 30 minutes, add additional stock if rice is dry and not yet tender. Serve with fresh green peas and braised celery.

PHEASANT LIVERS—*Italian Style*

Sauté ½ lb. pheasant (or other bird livers) in butter. Combine with 1 quart of Italian tomato sauce (see Chap. IV) Serve over spaghetti or rice.

Kidney

Remove covering membrane, soak in cold salted water for 30 to 60 minutes, depending on the size. Kidneys from a young animal should be cooked very briefly—kidneys the size of a beef kidney (about 1 lb.) may be browned and added to a stew.

SAUTEED KIDNEYS

3 or 4 small kidneys   Pepper
¼ cup butter   Marjoram
1 tbsp. minced onion   Juice of ½ lemon

Cut the kidneys in thin slices, sauté gently with onion in butter until they begin to brown. Add pepper, marjoram and lemon juice and simmer one or two minutes more. Serve over rice or with corn meal dumplings (see Chap. XII).

STEAK AND KIDNEY PIE

This hearty old English dish is perfect for winter appetites.

1½ lbs. round steak (deer, moose or elk)
¾ lb. kidney (beef kidney may be substituted if game kidneys have already been used)
   Flour seasoned with salt and pepper
2 tsps. parsley flakes
   Generous sprinkle of thyme and rosemary
3 tbsps. fat or drippings
3 or 4 carrots, cut in ½" slices
3 or 4 stalks of celery, cut in ½" slices
1 large onion, sliced
3 cups stock or beef bouillon

Remove white center and tubes from kidney and any gristle or connective tissue from round steak. Cut both in 1" cubes and dredge with seasoned flour. Brown slowly in hot fat in heavy skillet or dutch oven. Brown only enough cubes at one time to be uncrowded in the bottom of the pan. When the meat is all browned, place vegetables in pan and brown these also, adding parsley, thyme, and rosemary at this time. Add bouillon or stock and stir vigorously, scraping the bottom of the pan to loosen all browned particles. Return meat to the pan, cover and simmer on very low flame until meat is nearly tender. Pour into large casserole or individual ones, top with pie crust, seal edges and cut gashes in the crust for steam to escape. Bake at 325° until crust is golden brown.

I have also used leftover mashed potatoes, whipped fluffy again with an egg and a bit of milk, as a crust.

Tongue

The tongue, like the heart, has received considerable exercise during the animal's life and therefore, needs long slow cooking to make it tender. If you are not planning on a head mount from your animal, remove the tongue, wash it and place it—skin and roots still on—in a kettle of cold water over a moderate fire while you go about skinning your animal. By the time you're ready for a break, the tongue will be ready for some further attention from you.

BOILED FRESH TONGUE

Assuming that the tongue has already been simmering for about an hour, drain off this water, rinse the kettle and the tongue and replace with fresh hot water to cover, adding 1 tsp. salt per quart of water. Add several whole cloves, 1 or 2 bay leaves, a few peppercorns, and an onion. Cover the kettle and simmer until the tongue is tender. For a small deer tongue, this may only take another hour or so—for a moose or elk tongue, the time required will probably be about 5 hours. When the tongue is tender, allow it to cool in the stock until you can handle it. While it is still warm, remove from the broth, slice off the root and trim any excess fat. The skin will peel off easily. Serve the tongue sliced, hot or cold—it will make marvelous sandwiches for the next day. And don't forget the lentil or pea soup that is an extra bonus on this deal. If you've been planning ahead, you probably have those legumes soaking already!

Moose Nose

Mrs. G. C. F. Dalziel of Watson Lake, Yukon gives a full account of the preparation of this Northern specialty.

"Moose nose is a great delicacy with the Telegraph Creek Indians. When I first cooked it twenty odd years ago, I thought someone was joking but tried it anyway and it turned out to be just as good as they said it would be.

"The only distasteful part of it is that the nose must be cooked for the first hour or so—complete with hide and hair—and to peek into the pot and see all that fur bubbling like a drowned muskrat will make you put the lid back on fast!

"After at least an hour of cooking, cool the nose till you can skin the hide off easily and wash off thoroughly with cold water. Return to a kettle of cold water to cover, add salt, ground pepper and a few bay leaves and boil till tender. Remove and chill. Serve chilled on toasted squares or crackers."

Heart

Heart requires long slow cooking with moist heat to be at its flavorful best. It cannot be hurried, but is well worth waiting for. Remove veins, arteries, connective tissue and fat. Rinse thoroughly in cold water.

BRAISED HEART

Slice heart ½" thick. In heavy skillet, brown 3 slices of diced bacon, along with celery, carrot, onion and parsley root, cut in small pieces. When vegetables are nearly browned, push to one side of skillet and brown heart lightly. Add just enough stock or water to cover and simmer covered until heart is fork tender. Put vegetables through a sieve and return to gravy, season to taste with salt and pepper, blend in 3 to 4 tbsps. sour cream and heat just to boiling point. Serve with noodles, rice or dumplings.

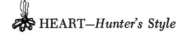 HEART—*Hunter's Style*

Slice heart ½" thick, roll in seasoned flour and brown slowly in butter or drippings. Add ½ package of dehydrated beef vegetable soup and 1½ cups water. Cover and simmer until heart is tender.

STUFFED HEART

Clean heart. Season inside and out with salt and pepper. Stuff with any favorite stuffing with either bread or rice as a base. Since the heart will be cooked by moist heat, keep the stuffing on the dry side and don't pack the cavity too full—allow room for the stuffing to expand. Sew or tie the heart together firmly and dredge with flour seasoned with a pinch of marjoram and rosemary. Brown in hot fat in dutch oven, add 1 cup stock or beef bouillon and simmer slowly until tender. Remove heart from dutch oven, thicken gravy with a flour and water paste, adding more stock or bouillon, if necessary. Stir over low flame until smooth and thick.

CHAPTER VIII

Planned Leftovers

GAME LEFTOVERS need present no problem to the ingenious housewife, especially now that freezers are in such common use. With a bit of foresight and imagination, the leftovers can be equally as delicious as the original dish.

I discovered long ago that cooking for two can be a bit difficult (as well as expensive) unless you develop a repertoire of what I call "planned leftovers." In my opinion, you can't cook a roast properly unless it's of fair size and there is a limit, especially in this household, to the number of times one can serve cold sliced roast. The same thing is true in most families, regardless of size.

I try to have at least some ideas in mind, and in many cases I do the advance preparation, before I tuck the leftovers away in the freezer. Then after the original dish has been forgotten, I can present the leftovers in a completely new guise. Leftovers have been the featured attraction at "company luncheons" and at the cocktail hour preceding a dinner party. No one has been aware of their humble origin.

Food frozen raw (such as game) can be safely refrozen when it has been cooked. However, the maximum time for freezer storage of leftovers is three months—so keep a record of leftovers that you have "squirreled away." Boiled potatoes and hard boiled eggs should not be included in dishes you plan to freeze—the potatoes become watery and the eggs tough and rubbery.

With a supply of stock from bones on hand and prepared soups in the cupboard to serve as the base for sauces, the flavor variations are limited only by your imagination. An extra flourish, such as fresh mushrooms or a bit of wine in a sauce, will help lift a casserole out of the ordinary. You'll still be ahead on your budget, for you've utilized the leftovers for another meal instead of giving them to the dog.

To save freezer space and to prevent freezer burn from air trapped inside oddly shaped packages, I usually cut meat from the bones immediately, dice it or grind it, and then pack it in plastic containers.

The gravy is frozen separately in small containers and then the two packages fastened together with freezer tape. Slices of breast meat from birds are wrapped in self-adhering plastic film with a double fold of waxed paper or film between slices, then sealed carefully in freezer paper or plastic bags.

Ground Meat or Fowl

CROQUETTES

2 cups ground leftover
  meat or fowl
½ cup chopped mushrooms,
  sautéed in butter
1 egg, beaten
½ cup bread crumbs
  Lemon juice or Worcestershire
    sauce

Minced onion
Chopped parsley or minced
celery
Sufficient white sauce, canned
soup, or gravy to moisten

Blend all the above ingredients together, seasoning to taste, and then chill for an hour or so before shaping into flat patties or the traditional cone shaped croquettes. Dip croquettes into beaten egg and then into crumbs, deep fry at 375°, or pan fry in hot melted butter. Serve with any savory sauce which will blend with the meat flavor.

PINWHEELS

Prepare biscuits, using 1 cup mix (see Chap. XII). Roll or pat dough into oblong shape on floured board a scant ½" thick. Spread with croquette mixture described above and roll up from the long side of the oblong. Cut thick slices and place on greased cookie sheet. Bake at 350° for 20 to 25 minutes, until biscuits are browned. Serve with gravy which has been extended with tomato, mushroom or cream of celery soup.

STUFFED VEGETABLES

Prepare vegetables for stuffing as described in Chap. IV.

Use croquette mixture or:

2 cups ground leftover
   meat or fowl

½ cup cooked rice

Chopped celery or green pepper

Minced onion

Salt and pepper to taste

Soup or gravy to moisten

Blend the above ingredients and proceed as in Chap. IV.

 HASH

2 cups coarsely ground or
   diced leftover meat

1 cup diced boiled potatoes

1 onion, chopped

Salt and pepper to taste

Chili sauce, catsup,
   or gravy to moisten

Toss lightly with a fork to blend. Place in heated well greased skillet, set over slow fire or in reflector oven to brown and heat through. If desired, form wells in top of hash with back of spoon, and when hash has begun to brown, crack an egg into each hollow, season with salt and pepper and cover skillet until the eggs are done to your liking.

TURNOVERS OR PASTIES

2 cups ground leftover pot roast

Minced onion

Chopped parsley

1 egg, beaten

Dash of Worcestershire sauce

Gravy to moisten

Pastry for double crust pie

Mix meat with seasonings, egg and gravy. Roll out pastry and cut into 5 or 6 inch rounds. Place a heaping tablespoon of meat mixture on one half of each round, fold the other half over and seal edges with the tines of a fork. Cut several slits for steam to escape, brush with beaten egg yolk or milk and bake on ungreased cooky sheet at 450° for 10 minutes, reduce heat to 350° and bake until golden brown (about 20 minutes). Serve hot with leftover gravy or mushroom sauce. These are also delicious made in miniature and served as hot canapes.

SANDWICH SPREAD

Coarsely ground meat or fowl

Chopped pickles or capers

Minced onion
Mayonnaise to moisten

Prepared mustard or anchovy
paste if the mixture needs
added zest

PHEASANT OR GROUSE MOUSSE

This is an elegant dish for a bridge luncheon—serves 4.

1 envelope (1 tbsp.)
    unflavored gelatine
¼ cup dry white wine
½ cup hot game bird stock
2 egg yolks
½ cup milk
1½ cups ground fowl
2 tbsps. mayonnaise
    Several sprigs parsley, chopped

6 to 8 green olives, sliced
1 stalk celery, finely diced or
    3 tbsps. slivered
    toasted almonds
Few drops lemon juice
Salt and pepper
Dash of onion salt
½ cup heavy cream

Soften gelatine in wine. Beat egg yolks in top of double boiler, add milk and set over hot (not boiling) water and stir constantly. Add hot stock slowly and continue to stir until the mixture coats the spoon. Remove from the hot water and stir in the gelatin and wine until dissolved. Cool until mixture begins to thicken. Oil 4 individual molds with salad oil and turn upside down to drain. Blend together ground fowl, mayonnaise, parsley, celery, lemon juice and seasonings. Fold into thickening gelatine mixture. Whip cream and fold in with a dash of paprika, if desired. Spoon into molds and chill until set. Unmold onto chilled plates and garnish with parsley, radish roses. Serve with hot rolls or cheese straws.

Diced Meat or Fowl

QUICK TOMATO GOULASH

1 lb. cubed leftover meat
2 tbsps. fat or drippings
1 cup water

1 8-oz. can tomato sauce
1 pkg. dehydrated
    vegetable soup mix

Brown leftover meat lightly in fat. Stir in remaining ingredients and simmer over slow fire until vegetables have become tender. An extra pinch of dried onion flakes might be added also.

CURRY

Particularly good with fowl, sheep or goat.

2 tbsps. butter	1 tbsp. curry powder
1 onion, minced	1 tsp. ginger
Coarsely grated lime rind,	2 cups stock, blended with
if available	2 tbsps. flour
Pinch of cardamon	2 cups leftover diced meat

Brown onion and lime in butter, add seasonings and simmer for 10 minutes on a low flame. Add stock and flour, stir and cook until thick and smooth. Add diced meat, check seasonings and heat thoroughly. Serve over fluffy rice.

PILAF

1 cup long grain rice, 2 sliced onions, butter, curry powder and cardamon if fowl is being used, or bay leaf or oregano if meat is being used, meat or bird stock or tomato juice, 2 to 3 cups diced leftover meat or fowl, Sautéed mushrooms, if desired.

Wash rice 6 times in hot water, 6 times in cold water and set aside to drain on paper towels. Brown sliced onions in large flameproof casserole in ¼ cup butter. Remove onions while you brown the rice in the same casserole. Stir the rice constantly, adding more butter as needed, until the rice is a golden color. Add seasonings and enough stock to cover the rice completely. Stir over the flame until the stock is bubbling, add the diced meat and onions and blend in. Cover the casserole and place in a 350° oven until the rice is tender and the liquid absorbed. If desired, add sautéed mushrooms just before serving, tossing lightly with a fork to blend.

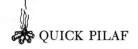 QUICK PILAF

2 to 3 cups leftover meat	Minced onion
or fowl, diced	2 cups canned tomatoes, cut up
3 cups cooked rice	1 cup gravy or stock

Combine all ingredients, season to taste and put in a greased casserole. Top with buttered crumbs and bake at moderate heat in reflector oven about ½ hour.

GAME PIES

2 cups diced meat or fowl	1 pkg. frozen peas,
1½ cups gravy or 1 cup stock,	thawed but not cooked
½ cup cream and 3 tbsps.	½ cup carrots, sliced and
roux blended together	parboiled 5 minutes
½ cup tiny whole onions,	½ cup mushrooms, sautéed
parboiled 5 minutes	in butter

Combine all ingredients, season to taste and pour into buttered casserole. Proceed as you wish:

1. Top with pastry, cut gashes for steam to escape, seal pastry to edge of casserole, bake at 400° until pastry is browned.
2. Cover casserole with a mashed potato crust—if desired, ½ cup grated sharp cheddar cheese may be blended into the potatoes.
3. Top with biscuits, bake at 375° for 45 minutes or until biscuits are brown.
4. Line individual pie plates (4″ to 5″ in diameter) with pastry. Use only enough gravy to moisten ingredients, divide the filling among the pastry lined pie plates, and cover with a top crust, crimping the edges and cutting gashes as you would for any pie. Bake at 400° until the crust is brown. Carefully loosen the edge of the pies and slide each one into a dinner plate. Pass remainder of the gravy hot in a separate sauce boat.

GAME BIRD SOUFFLE

Make a heavy white sauce of the following and cool: 4 tbsps. butter, 4 tbsps. flour, 1 cup milk.

4 egg yolks	Cayenne or curry
1 cup finely diced fowl	Grated onion to taste
Salt and pepper	4 egg whites, stiffly beaten
Celery salt	

Add egg yolks to white sauce, one at a time, beating vigorously after each addition. Add fowl and seasonings to taste, then gently fold in egg whites. Spoon into buttered souffle dish, set in a pan of hot water and bake at 350° for 45 minutes. Serve immediately with green salad and hot rolls. 4 servings.

15 MINUTE SUPPER—*Chinese Style*

1 lb. diced leftover meat or fowl
2 tbsps. oil or butter
2 tbsps. soy sauce
1 cup stock or ½ cup stock
    and ½ cup gravy
½ cup minced onion
1 lb. can Chinese vegetables,
    drained

1 tbsp. cornstarch
¼ tsp. ginger
1 tbsp. honey or light molasses
¼ cup dry sherry or water

Brown meat lightly in butter, add soy sauce, stock, onion and vegetables. Simmer 5 to 8 minutes, only until thoroughly heated. Meanwhile, combine cornstarch, ginger, honey and sherry and add to skillet, stirring only until thickened and clear. Serve over rice or crisp Chinese noodles.

Sliced Meats

Serve Apricot sauce (see Chap. X) with cold sliced game birds. Serve Cumberland sauce or Viennese game sauce (see Chap. X) with cold sliced roast venison.

PHEASANT OR TURKEY DIVAN

Butter a shallow oven proof casserole. Place in it slices of pheasant or wild turkey breast meat, top each slice with a thin slice of boiled ham. Cook broccoli or asparagus until tender, but still crisp, and place several stalks of asparagus or one larger piece of broccoli on each portion. Cover with 2 cups rich cream sauce to which has been added ¼ cup Parmesan cheese and a whisper of minced onion, sprinkle with another spoon or two of cheese. Place in 350° oven for 15 minutes and then slide briefly under the broiler until the sauce is bubbly and brown.

Pates

These are all more or less interchangeable and will vary in flavor according to the game used. I have listed several to show how practically identical results may be obtained by different methods.

TERRINE DE FOIE DE VENAISON

2 lbs. uncooked venison liver
½ lb. pork fat
¾ lb. lean leftover
    venison roast
1 tbsp. brandy
    Juice of a lemon
    Generous grating of nutmeg

Generous pinch of thyme
Thin slices of fat pork back

Using the fine blade, put the liver, pork fat and venison through the food chopper twice. Add brandy, lemon juice and seasonings and work to a smooth paste. Line a terrine or earthenware dish with thin slices of fat pork back, then pack in the pâté mixture and cover with additional slices of pork back. Cover the terrine and set in a boiling water bath almost to the top of the mold. Bake 2 hours at 375°. Drain off liquid fat, weigh down and chill. Serve cold—or reheat, slice and serve with a zesty tomato sauce.

HASENPASTETE

½ lb. leftover rabbit meat
1 tbsp. butter
2 tsp. minced onion
2 whole eggs plus 1 egg white,
    beaten well
⅓ cup dry breadcrumbs

Salt and pepper to taste
Rabbit stock

Put rabbit meat through food chopper twice, using fine blade. Combine with other ingredients, adding only enough stock to moisten it—it should not be too liquid. Butter a small mold liberally, sprinkle with fine dry crumbs and fill with rabbit mixture. Cover mold with waxed paper and foil, tie securely and steam for 1 hour. Turn out of mold and chill. Serve with thinly sliced buttered toast.

HIRSCHPASTETE

½ lb. leftover venison   2 tsps. finely minced onion
1 slice bread   Pinch thyme
¼ lb. butter   1 tbsp. Madeira wine
2 eggs, beaten   Salt and pepper to taste

Grind the venison and bread together twice, using the fine blade on the food chopper. Work into a smooth paste with the butter, eggs and seasonings. Steam for 1 hour in a greased covered mold—then chill. OR Roll out puff paste, fill with pate, fold over and seal. Bake at 400° for 15 minutes, lower heat to 300° and bake until puff paste is golden and crisp.

GAME BIRD PATE

Remove the skin of cooked game birds and bone. Grind the meat twice, using fine blade of food chopper. Leftover bird livers and giblets may be included. In the proportion of ½ lb. fowl to ¼ lb. butter, work the two to a smooth paste. Season to taste with salt and pepper, mace or ginger. Pack firmly in a small casserole and place in a slow oven to heat through. Press down again after it is heated, cover with clarified butter and chill.

LIVER PASTE

½ lb. leftover sautéed liver   Dash cayenne
1 tbsp. butter   2 tbsps. lemon juice
1 tbsp. onion juice   Bit of prepared mustard,
1 tsp. celery salt   if desired

Grind the liver twice, using fine blade of food chopper. Work in butter and seasonings until it is a smooth paste. Pack in small jars and use as a spread for canapes. Or see Chap. XI for Pâté in aspic.

CHAPTER IX

Garnishes and other Game Accompaniments

GAME IS SUCH A LUXURY in itself that it needs little in the way of embellishment. Some garnishes and accompaniments are traditional however, and not only enhance and complement the flavor of the game, but please the eye as well.

Fruits and tart fruit jellies have a natural affinity for game. Often, they are used in the cooking of the meat itself or are added to the sauce. A few bright sprigs of parsley or watercress and a well-chosen fruit garnish, where appropriate, will add a festive touch to the platter without that "gussied-up" look most men detest.

Fruit Garnishes

GLAZED ORANGES

2 cups sugar	2 tbsps. lemon juice
1 cup water	3 or 4 large seedless oranges

Combine sugar, water and lemon juice in a large skillet. Bring to a boil on low heat and then simmer for 5 minutes. Meanwhile, wash oranges and cut fairly thick slices, leaving the skin on. Poach the orange slices gently in the syrup, turning at least once, until the skin of the oranges is transparent. Cool in the syrup and drain just before serving. A flavor variation may be achieved by adding a few whole cloves or a small piece of dried ginger root to the syrup. Place a whole clove or a candied cranberry in the center of each slice, if desired.

GLAZED APPLE RINGS

2 cups sugar	6 large firm apples

1½ cups water or
    cranberry juice
¼ cup lemon juice

2 pieces stick cinnamon,
    if desired
2 or 3 whole cloves, if desired

Wash and core apples, slice unpeeled into fairly thick slices. Place in large flat baking pan, and cover with remaining ingredients which have been boiled together for 5 minutes. Bake apple slices at 275° to 300° until apples are transparent, basting occasionally with syrup. These slices may be prepared in large quantities and frozen for later use. Pack into plastic containers with a double fold of waxed paper between the layers. They may also be served as dessert with vanilla ice cream or a boiled custard.

QUICK SPICED FRUIT

1 lb. can whole apricots,
    crab apples or pears
⅓ cup lemon juice or
    cider vinegar if you prefer

6 tbsps. sugar
Dozen whole cloves
2 sticks cinnamon

Drain the juice from the canned fruit, combine with sugar, lemon and spices and simmer 15 minutes. Pour over fruit and let it stand in the refrigerator for several days. If I have fresh lemons on hand, I very often add a few thin slices of lemon to the syrup.

PEARS POACHED WITH CRANBERRIES

Add 1 cup fresh or frozen cranberries to the syrup from a can of pears. Simmer until the skins pop, but do not cook so long that the berries become mushy. Skim the berries out with a slotted spoon and set aside. Gently poach the pears until they have acquired a rosy hue, turning at least once in the syrup. To serve, place the cranberries in the centers of the pear halves.

SAUTEED FRUIT

Canned peach halves, pineapple rings or apricot halves may be drained well, then sautéed in butter until they are delicately browned. Sprinkle with a bit of brown sugar and a light dash of curry powder, if desired, before serving.

Fruit Relishes and Jellies

RAW CRANBERRY RELISH

4 cups fresh or frozen cranberries
2 oranges
1 lemon
1 lime, if available

1 cup granulated sugar (or more, if you prefer it quite sweet)

Using the medium blade of the food chopper, grind the cranberries and the quartered and seeded citrus fruits, including the fruit peels. Mix well and add sugar to your taste. We prefer it not too sweet, especially when served with fowl. Allow the relish to mellow in the refrigerator for at least several hours. This is also delicious served over vanilla ice cream as a change from too-rich desserts, especially at holiday time.

RAW BLUEBERRY RELISH

The above recipe may also be used with blueberries, either fresh or frozen by the dry pack method. A little less sugar will be needed, as blueberries are quite sweet in comparison to cranberries.

(Both cranberries and blueberries are delightful all year round, and extremely versatile. When they are available in the market, purchase extra packages and freeze them, as is. When ready to use them, pick them over while still frozen, then wash and use them immediately, just as you would fresh ones.)

SPICED CRANBERRY SAUCE

Cook together for 5 minutes:
1½ cups water
1 orange, including juice
   and finely chopped rind
2 cups sugar
1 piece stick cinnamon

Add:
4 cups fresh or frozen
   cranberries

Cook until berries stop popping. Cool without stirring.

BAKED CRANBERRY RELISH

4 cups cranberries   Juice of 1 lemon or lime
2 cups sugar
¾ cup toasted slivered almonds
1 cup citrus fruit marmalade

Combine washed and drained cranberries with sugar and place in a shallow pan, cover tightly and bake at 350° for 1 hour. Combine cranberries with remaining ingredients, mix well and chill.

WILD CURRANT JELLY

I have been delighted to find currants growing wild right here on our land. They are seldom seen in the markets in urban areas any more, since they are so easily crushed and bruised by handling. When picking currants for jelly, include some that are not completely ripe, as the pectin and acid content will be higher. If you use all ripe berries, then add liquid commercial pectin.

To extract the juice, combine 4 lbs. red currants with 1 cup water in saucepan. Crush the fruit thoroughly and simmer covered for 10 minutes. Strain through a jelly bag for several folds of cheesecloth, wrung out of hot water. Measure the juice.

If some unripe fruit has been included, proceed as follows: Add ¾ cup granulated sugar for each cup of juice in a large saucepan. Stir until the sugar is dissolved and then boil rapidly until the jelly stage is reached. With currants, it will be only a few minutes until two drops of the jelly will hang from the side of the spoon. Skim and pour at once into hot sterilized glasses. Seal with paraffin.

If you are using all ripe fruit, proceed in this way:

5 cups juice
7 cups sugar
½ bottle liquid
    commercial pectin

Combine juice and sugar in a very large kettle, heat over high heat, stirring constantly until boiling. Add pectin, bring to a full rolling boil and boil hard for 1 minute, stirring constantly. Remove from fire, skim quickly and pour into hot sterilized glasses. Seal with paraffin.

GOOSEBERRY SAUCE

Delicious with venison as well as boar

1 quart gooseberries
   Juice and grated rind
      of 1 lemon or orange,
      plus enough water
      to make a total
      of 2 cups liquid

1 piece stick cinnamon
2 or 3 whole cloves

Combine liquid, cinnamon and cloves and boil together for 15 minutes. Add washed gooseberries and simmer gently until tender. Remove gooseberries with a slotted spoon, take out spices, reduce syrup by half and pour over gooseberries.

CHOKECHERRY JELLY

My introduction to chokecherries was a rude one—purple-footed dogs and people the summer we moved to the Midwest. Since then, I have discovered the delicious jelly they provide, in addition to food for the birds, so I now hold them in much higher esteem.

3½ lbs. chokecherries
3 cups water
3 cups juice
6½ cups sugar
1 bottle liquid commercial
    pectin
   Simmer crushed berries in
    water covered for 15
    minutes.

Strain through a jelly bag
and measure the juice.

Mix sugar and juice in a very large kettle over high heat. Bring to a boil, stirring constantly. Add pectin and bring to a full rolling boil and hard for 1 minute, stirring constantly. Remove from flame, skim and pour into hot sterilized glasses at once. Seal with hot paraffin.

Hint To Busy Housewives: If you're too busy to make jelly when the fruit is ready, extract the juice and store it in quart containers in the freezer until you have a bit more leisure.

PARSLEY JELLY

Remove the stalks and wash thoroughly several large bunches of parsley. Place in enamel saucepan and cover with water. Bring to a boil and then simmer for ½ to ¾ hour. Strain through jelly bag and measure juice. Combine sugar and juice, cup for cup, and boil, stirring constantly until jelly "sheets." Add ½ tsp. lemon extract for each cup of jelly, pour into hot sterilized glasses and seal.

ORANGE HERB JELLY

Wash and crush ½ cup fresh marjoram leaves (or use ¼ cup dried marjoram leaves). Combine with 1 cup water, bring to a boil and then simmer covered for 5 to 10 minutes. Strain thru a jelly bag or very fine sieve and measure the juice. Combine with enough water to make one cup and place in large saucepan with 3¼ cups sugar. Stirring constantly, bring to a boil and boil hard for 1 minute. Remove from heat, add 1 6-oz. can thawed orange juice concentrate and ¼ cup strained lemon juice. Add ½ bottle liquid pectin and mix well. Skim and pour at once into hot sterilized glasses.

GRAPEFRUIT AND SAVORY JELLY

Infuse savory leaves as directed in the preceding recipe. Measure the strained juice and add enough canned grapefruit juice to make a total of 2 cups. Combine with 3½ cups sugar in large saucepan and bring to a boil, stirring constantly. Add ½ bottle pectin, then bring to a full rolling boil and boil hard for 1 minute, stirring constantly. Remove from flame, skim, and pour at once into hot sterilized glasses. Seal with hot paraffin.

APPLE AND SAGE JELLY

This may be made in the exact manner of grapefruit and savory, using bottled apple juice.

The flavor of these herb jellies is subtle and different—they are particularly suited to game, but may be used with any meat or poultry.

Garnishes for Small Birds

ROUENNAISE

Brown the bird liver in butter for 2 or 3 minutes, season with thyme and salt and pepper, add a dash of sherry or brandy and cook an additional 1 to 2 minutes. Mash to a smooth paste and spread on croutons.

There is no reason not to enjoy this delicacy in camp. Sauté the bird livers gently in butter or margarine with a pinch of seasoning and perhaps a whiff of dried onion flakes. Do it over a slow part of the fire while the birds are broiling and the toast is browning. Put one whole liver on each piece of crisp toast, divide up the butter and drippings from the bird on the toast slices. It only takes a few minutes for the livers to be lightly browned, yet tender enough to be mashed to a paste on the toast.

CROUTONS

Trim crusts from bread with a very sharp knife, cut into cubes, diamonds or shapes to fit the birds or filets. They may be fried in butter or just toasted in the oven. However, I prefer to brush the croutons liberally with melted butter and toast them on a flat baking sheet in a 300° oven until delicately brown and very crisp. Herb croutons may be made by adding a pinch of finely crushed dry herbs or finely chopped fresh ones to the melted butter. Two pleasing combinations for rather bland dishes would be chervil and thyme or tarragon and parsley.

Soup Garnishes

WIENER ERBSEN—*Viennese Peas*

Heat fat for deep frying to 375°. Make a batter as follows: Beat 1 egg with 2 tbsps. milk and a pinch of salt. Add all at once to ¾ cup flour and beat smooth. Dip tip of small spoon into hot fat and drop tiny balls of batter into hot fat. Cook until golden (only a minute or so), remove from fat and drain on paper towels.

CUSTARD CUBES FOR CONSOMME

⅓ cup milk or game stock,   1 egg, slightly beaten with a
   scalded   pinch of salt and paprika

Slowly pour scalded liquid into egg, stirring rapidly as you pour.
Strain thru cheesecloth or a fine sieve into a small shallow pan. Set
in a larger pan on oven rack, fill outer pan with boiling water. Bake
about 30 minutes at 325° or until custard is set. Cool, cut into cubes
or fancy shapes and add to soup when ready to serve.

GAME QUENELLES

½ lb. uncooked game   Salt and pepper
½ cup heavy cream   2 egg whites, stiffly beaten

Put the meat through a food chopper twice, using fine blade. Season
to taste and work in heavy cream. Chill for an hour or so, and then
add egg whites. Form in small balls and poach gently in boiling
stock for 10 to 15 minutes.

OR:

½ lb. cooked and finely   Salt and pepper
   ground game   2 tbsps. cream
¼ cup butter   Paste of ¼ cup water,
1 egg plus 1 egg yolk   1 tbsp. butter, 2 tbsps. flour

Combine all ingredients and work into a smooth paste. Season to
taste and chill for an hour. Shape into small balls and poach gently
in boiling stock.

LEBERKNÖDEL

½ lb. venison liver   1 small clove garlic,
1 cup boiling water   minced (may be omitted)
1 egg   1 tbsp. butter
⅓ cup cream   Several sprigs parsley, chopped
1 cup fine dry breadcrumbs   Pinch marjoram
¼ cup minced onion   Salt and pepper to taste

Simmer liver in boiling water for 5 minutes, drain and remove membrane and tubes. Put through medium blade of food chopper. Beat egg with cream, blend in bread crumbs. Add onion and garlic which have been sautéed briefly in butter. Add liver and seasonings and blend well. Shape into 1″ balls and cook in boiling water or stock. Cook only a few at a time and remove as they rise to the surface. Serve several dumplings in each bowl of soup. Any remaining may be frozen for several weeks.

CHAPTER X

Sauces and Stuffings

SAUCES

An entire book could be written on sauces alone. The French consider sauce making the high point of their cuisine and the saucier rules supreme in the kitchen. However, it is not my intent to compete with Escoffier and I have included here only a few of the thousands of flavor combinations possible—those most suited to game cookery.

Discretion should be the watchword in making and serving sauces. Use seasonings subtly to achieve sauces that are neither too bland nor too blatant—herbs and spices add much to a sauce, but should never dominate. Serve sauces with the same restraint—vegetables with sauce combine well with simple broiled meats or fish, while meats served with sauce require vegetables dressed only with butter and seasoning.

Sauces fall into two main categories—white and brown—both of which use a roux, or blend of butter and flour, as the base. Brown sauce is the foundation of most highly seasoned and savory sauces and is made with the venison stock (or beef stock) described in Chap. II. White sauces are made with milk, cream and/or stock from fowl, as described in Chap. II, or fish stock. These are usually more delicate in flavor.

Roux may be made up in quantity and stored in a covered container in the refrigerator, to be used as needed to thicken gravies and sauces.

ROUX FOR GRAVIES AND SAUCES

½ cup butter   ½ cup flour

Melt butter over low flame, blend in flour gradually and stir constantly until the mixture is smooth and bubbly. If the roux is not allowed to darken at all, it may be used for the most delicate of white sauces, as well as for thickening all gravies. This amount makes ¾ cup of roux and is used as follows:

When recipe calls for 1 tbsp. butter and 1 tbsp. flour, use 1½ tbsps. roux. 2 tbsps. butter and 2 tbsps. flour, use 3 tbsps. roux.

The roux may be reheated in a double boiler over hot water and the liquid added slowly, or the roux may be added directly to the warm liquid, as in a fricassee gravy. In either case, constant stirring over a low flame will produce a smooth sauce.

If a brown roux is desired, combine ½ cup butter, ¾ cup flour.

Proceed as above, but continue to cook, stirring constantly until a rich brown color is achieved. The larger amount of flour is necessary, as flour loses some of its thickening power as it is browned.

White Sauces

BASIC WHITE SAUCE

Thin: 1½ tbsps. roux, 1 cup milk, salt and pepper to taste. Medium: 3 tbsps. roux, 1 cup milk, salt and pepper to taste. Thick: 4½ tbsps. roux, 1 cup milk, salt and pepper to taste. Add milk slowly to melted roux, stir constantly over low flame or in double boiler until smooth and thickened. Season to taste.

BECHAMEL SAUCE—*for fowl and vegetables*

1 cup strong broth
  (game bird or chicken)
1 slice onion
  Few peppercorns
4½ tbsps. roux
1 cup milk
  Salt to taste

1 egg yolk, if desired

Simmer the stock with onion and peppercorns for 10 minutes, then strain. Melt the roux, slowly add broth, then milk, stirring constantly until thickened. Season to taste with salt. If desired, the egg yolk may be beaten with a few spoons of the hot sauce, then slowly added to the sauce, stirring vigorously. Do not allow the sauce to boil once the egg yolk has been added.

ALLEMANDE SAUCE—*for vegetables*

1 cup white sauce, made	1 tbsp. cream
with half stock, half cream	Pinch nutmeg
1 egg yolk	1½ tsp. lemon juice

Reduce the white sauce by half over a low flame, set over hot water and slowly add beaten egg yolk, stirring vigorously. Add cream, nutmeg and lemon juice, stirring until thick and creamy.

CAPER SAUCE—*for fish, sheep or cold meats*

4½ tbsps. roux	Salt and pepper to taste
1½ cups stock in which	
meat or fish was cooked	

Combine roux, stock and seasonings and simmer, stirring constantly until thick, or use 1½ cups bechamel sauce. Add:

2 tbsps. butter	1 tsp. lemon juice
3 tbsps. capers	

Continue to stir over low heat until well blended.

CHEESE SAUCE—*for fish, vegetables, or leftover game birds*

1 cup white or bechamel sauce	Bit of grated onion, if desired
(made with the appropriate	Dash of cayenne pepper
stock)	
¼ cup grated cheddar, swiss	
or Parmesan cheese	

Stir over low flame until cheese is melted and well blended.

CUCUMBER SAUCE—*for boiled fish*

1 cup white sauce or bechamel	Dash of paprika
(made with fish stock)	½ to ¾ cup peeled and
1½ tsp. lemon juice	finely diced raw cucumber

DILL SAUCE—*for vegetables or fish*

1 cup white sauce
½ cup sour cream
1 tbsp. freshly snipped dill leaves

1 tsp. grated onion
1 tbsp. chopped parsley

Combine over low heat, but do not allow to boil once sour cream has been added.

HORSERADISH SAUCE—*for boiled fish, sheep or goat, tongue*

1 cup white sauce
4 to 5 tbsps. drained horseradish

1 tbsp. butter

Combine white sauce and horseradish, heat and blend thoroughly. Add butter bit by bit just before serving.

MADEIRA SAUCE—*for game or poultry*

½ cup scalded cream
  Salt and pepper
½ cup Madeira

OR: 1½ tbsps. roux
    ½ cup game bird or vegetable stock
    ½ cup Madeira

Combine roux and stock or cream and stir over low heat until boiling point is reached. Season to taste and *slowly*, stirring constantly, add Madeira. Cook slowly another minute or so.

MUSHROOM SAUCE—*for game birds or fish*

1 cup white or bechamel sauce
½ cup mushrooms, sautéed in butter with 1 tsp. minced onion and 1 tsp. chopped parsley

WHITE WINE SAUCE—*for broiled game birds*

1½ tbsps. roux
1 cup strong game bird stock
1 cup cream
  Grating of fresh nutmeg

Salt and pepper
2 tbsps. white wine
1 tbsp. butter

Combine and stir over low flame roux, stock and cream. Stir until thickened and smooth, season to taste, add white wine and butter, cook only a minute or so until blended.

Brown Sauces

BASIC BROWN SAUCE

3 tbsps. brown roux   (or beef stock)
1 cup venison stock   Salt and pepper

Combine roux and stock and cook over low flame until smooth and thickened—about 5 minutes. Season to taste with salt and pepper.

BIGARADE SAUCE—*for venison and duck*

Julienne strips of orange   Juice of 1 orange
    peel from 2 oranges   1 tsp. lemon juice
2 cups brown sauce   Salt and pepper

Boil peel in water to cover for 5 minutes and then drain. Add to brown sauce and simmer until peel is tender. Add lemon and orange juices and season to taste. Heat until piping hot.

BORDELAISE SAUCE—*for venison steaks and chops*

Bacon or salt pork,   2 shallots
    several slices   6 to 8 peppercorns
2 carrots, sliced   Dash of cayenne
2 onions, sliced   1 clove garlic
    Sprig of thyme   1 tbsp. brown sauce
1 bay leaf   1 cup venison stock
1 cup claret or Bordeaux

Combine bacon, carrots, onions, thyme and bayleaf in pan and allow to simmer slowly in their own juices for 15 or 20 minutes. Add wine, shallots, peppercorns and garlic and continue to simmer gently until sauce is reduced and is brown and sticky. Add brown sauce and stock, bring to the boiling point, skim any fat that rises to the surface and strain through a sieve. Reduce further by ⅓ by slow cooking.

CURRY SAUCE—*for leftover meats, fish, or vegetables*

1 cup brown sauce
1 tbsp. minced onion,
    browned in butter

1 tsp. curry powder
1 tsp. tomato paste

MUSHROOM BROWN SAUCE— *for broiled venison, smoked meats*

1 cup brown sauce
½ cup fresh mushrooms, sautéed in butter with minced parsley

RAISIN SAUCE—*for tongue or boar*

Carmelize 1 tsp. granulated sugar over low flame, add 1 tsp. vinegar and stir until sugar is dissolved and sirupy. Add 1 cup brown sauce and ⅓ cup raisins, plumped in hot water and then drained.

Wine Sauces

APRICOT GAME SAUCE—*for cold game birds*

Blend together:
Small glass apricot marmalade
Juice of ½ lemon and grated rind

½ glass white wine
French mustard to taste
    (1 to 2 tsps.)

CHERRY SAUCE—*for quail and other small game birds*

½ cup veal or chicken stock
½ wineglass port
    Shredded lemon peel

3 tbsps. red currant jelly
½ cup sour cherry compote
1 tbsp. lemon juice

Simmer stock, port and peel in pan in which birds were cooked for 8 to 10 minutes. Add jelly, cherries and lemon juice and simmer another 3 minutes.

CUMBERLAND SAUCE—*for roast venison (all antlered game)*

1 cup red currant jelly
1 wineglass port
Juice of 1 lemon
½ tsp. ginger

Juice and shredded
  rind of 1 orange
1 tsp. dry mustard

Melt jelly with wine, reduce slightly, add juices and rind, seasonings and simmer 10 minutes.

ITALIAN GAME BIRD SAUCE

2 tbsps. butter
3 tbsps. minced onion
¼ cup chopped mushrooms
2 tsps. flour
Grating of fresh nutmeg

1 tbsp. tomato puree
½ cup white wine
½ cup game bird stock
1 tsp. herb blend for fowl

Sauté onion and mushrooms in butter, add flour and blend until smooth. Add nutmeg, puree, wine and stock and simmer 10 minutes. Blend in herbs and serve.

RUSSIAN GAME SAUCE—*for elk and venison*

2 tbsp. butter
¼ cup grated onion
1 cup dry white wine

1 pint sour cream
Salt and pepper

In small saucepan, melt butter and cook onion slowly until transparent, but not browned. Add wine and simmer until only ¼ cup wine remains. Slowly stir in sour cream and continue stirring until sauce just reaches boiling point. Season to taste with salt and pepper, strain through a sieve and serve very hot.

VIENNESE GAME SAUCE—*for venison*

2 tbsps. sour pitted
  cherry compote
⅓ cup red wine
⅓ cup venison stock

1 tbsp. toasted breadcrumbs
Shredded peel and
  juice of 1 lemon

Combine all ingredients and boil for 2 minutes.

And Other Game Sauces

BREAD SAUCE—*classic English sauce for grouse or partridge*

1 cup milk
1 small onion
1 whole clove
1 blade mace
2 oz. soft breadcrumbs (2 slices)
1 tbsp. butter, in 2 portions
1 tbsp. cream
Salt and pepper

In double boiler, slowly bring milk to scalding point with mace and onion into which clove has been stuck. Simmer 10 minutes and then remove onion and mace. Beat in crumbs with a whisk. Add salt and pepper to taste and half the butter. Cook for 10 minutes, stirring constantly. Add cream and rest of butter and blend well.

CREOLE SAUCE—*for meat, fish, shellfish, poultry and game*

This sauce is so versatile that I usually make a good quantity and freeze it.

½ cup butter
2 onions, minced
2 green peppers, minced
1 cup mushrooms
2 cups stock
1 quart canned tomatoes
Salt and pepper
Cayenne
Bay leaf
Thyme

¼ cup minced ham

Sauté onion, peppers, mushrooms in butter for 5 to 8 minutes. Add remaining ingredients and simmer 30 minutes. Add a bit of roux, if necessary to thicken.

Barbecue Sauces

BARNEY'S BARBECUE SAUCE—*for boar chops or ribs*

1 tsp. dry mustard   ½ tsp. cloves
1 tbsp. flour   ¼ cup vinegar
1 tsp. celery salt   ¼ cup water
½ tsp. cayenne   ½ cup catsup

Blend all ingredients together and simmer 10 minutes.

BARBECUE SAUCE II—*for bear, boar or ribs*

1 cup chili sauce   1 tsp. pepper
   (see recipe which follows)   1 tsp. chili powder
¼ cup vinegar   Dash cayenne
2 tbsps. Worcestershire sauce   1½ cups water
1 tsp. salt

Combine all ingredients and simmer together for 10 minutes.

BARBECUE SAUCE III—*for boar or tongue*

¾ cup catsup   2 tbsps. butter
2 tsps. prepared mustard   1 chopped green pepper
2 tbsps. sugar   1 chopped onion
   Dash Worcestershire sauce   ½ cup chopped pickles
½ cup vinegar   1 tsp. lemon juice

Brown the green pepper and onion in butter, add pickles and the
remaining ingredients which have been simmering together for 10
minutes. Cook for an additional 5 minutes.

OLD-FASHIONED CHILI SAUCE

(for meat loaf, as a 'burger garnish, with meats other than game)

This is my Grandmother's recipe which has been handed down without
change. It's as much a part of my childhood memories as the Christmas
pudding and the English fruitcake. The whole family joined in the
preparation of all of them.

1 peck red ripe tomatoes
4 large green sweet peppers
2 large red sweet peppers
6 large onions
2 cups vinegar

4 level tbsps. salt
5 to 6 cups light brown
   sugar, packed
1 large bunch celery

In a cheesecloth or muslin bag, combine the following:

2 tsps. ground ginger
4 tsps. cinnamon
2 tsps. cloves

2 tsps. allspice
4 tsps. grated nutmeg

Scald, peel, and cut up the tomatoes, put them on to boil while you chop the onions, celery and peppers. Add vegetables, vinegar, salt and sugar. Do not make the spice bag too small or the flavor will not come out, but tie it tightly or the spices will make the chili sauce dark. (I usually tie one end of the string from the spice bag to the handle of my big kettle.) Simmer for at least 2 hours over a very low flame, and stir often as it burns very easily. Pour into hot sterilized jars and seal. This should give you 6 or 7 quarts of chili sauce.

SEASONED BUTTERS

These are prepared by working the flavoring ingredients into butter at room temperature and then chilling.

ANCHOVY BUTTER: 1 part anchovy to 3 parts butter

GARLIC BUTTER: pound 1 clove garlic in mortar, combine with ¼ cup butter

LEMON BUTTER: ½ cup butter, 1 tbsp. chopped parsley, salt, pepper and cayenne to taste, 1 tbsp. lemon juice

MINT BUTTER: ¼ cup each chopped mint and butter, 1 tbsp. lemon juice

PAPRIKA BUTTER: 2 tsps. paprika to 2 tbsps. butter

SAVORY BUTTER: 2 tbsps. butter, ½ tsp. each, freshly chopped: parsley, chervil, tarragon, chives, shallot

WATERCRESS BUTTER: 1 tbsp. chopped watercress to 3 tbsps. butter

TARRAGON BUTTER: 1 tsp. fresh tarragon to 2 tbsps. butter

STUFFINGS

Stuffing adds its flavor to meat and poultry, at the same time absorbing some of the flavor of the meat. Stuffings should therefore be chosen with care to provide the maximum in flavor.

Fruit stuffings, especially when they are tart or slightly acid, are excellent with rich and rather fat meats or birds—goose, boar, muskrat. Stuffings for lean and somewhat drier meats and birds may be more rich and savory.

Stuffings expand considerably during the cooking process, so always stuff lightly to avoid a soggy mass of stuffing or a burst bird. Extra stuffing, especially when small birds are used, may be baked in a buttered casserole to provide extra servings.

When using bread as a base for stuffing, use bread that is at least a day old and slightly dry. Always toss ingredients lightly together with a fork to blend or you will have a soggy stuffing to start with. Birds or meats to be braised are often stuffed and here it is most important to start with a stuffing drier than usual. The steam generated in the braising kettle will moisten the stuffing to a great extent.

Regardless of what you may have read elsewhere, *never* stuff meats or fowl until you are ready to cook them. If you wish to make advance preparations, get your stuffing ingredients ready the day before—dice or crumb the bread, cook the rice, shell and peel chestnuts, steam prunes, etc. But do wait until you're ready to light the oven before you assemble the stuffing and fill the birds. (The only exception to this rule is the apple, onion or celery placed inside duck cavities to draw out any possible fishy taste.) After all, you are preparing a feast and you don't want it to turn into a disaster because of the development of dangerous toxins due to bacterial growth.

As a general rule, one cup of stuffing is figured on for each pound of bird, so adjust these recipes to the birds on hand and allow a bit extra to serve with them for second helpings.

Bread Stuffings

SAGE AND ONION STUFFING

3 quarts day old breadcrumbs	Salt and pepper to taste
½ to ¾ cup melted butter	2 tsps. crumbled sage
6 large stalks celery. diced	¾ tsp. thyme
3 large onions, chopped	½ tsp. rosemary

or
1½ tbsps. poultry seasoning in
    place of the last 3
    ingredients.

Melt butter over low flame in large skillet and cook onion and celery for 10 minutes without browning. Remove from heat and add breadcrumbs and seasonings. Toss lightly with a fork to blend and check seasonings, adding more if you wish. If you prefer a moister dressing, add a bit of broth. Sufficient for a 10 to 12 lb. turkey.

    Giblets, chopped—½ lb. mushrooms, sautéed in butter— ½ pint drained and chopped oysters may be added for flavor variations.

APPLE AND RAISIN STUFFING

¼ cup butter
1 quart breadcrumbs
⅔ cup raisins
3 diced apples
1 cup diced celery
½ cup coarsely broken nut
    meats, if desired

Pinch each of thyme and
    marjoram
Salt and pepper to taste
Apple juice or cider to moisten

Cook celery in melted butter for 5 minutes without browning. Add remaining ingredients, toss lightly to blend, season to taste and add cider or apple juice to moisten if necessary. Makes about 6 cups stuffing.

CRANBERRY STUFFING

2 cups coarsely chopped
    cranberries
½ cup sugar
½ cup butter
½ cup chopped celery
2 tbsps. minced onion

¼ cup snipped parsley
1 tsp. marjoram or ½ tsp.
    each thyme and marjoram
Salt and pepper to taste
2 quarts coarse breadcrumbs
Water or white wine to moisten

Combine chopped cranberries and sugar, let stand for ½ hour. Sauté gently in butter celery, onion and parsley for 5 minutes. Combine all ingredients and season to taste. Add wine or water to moisten slightly.

CHESTNUT STUFFING

2 cups chestnuts, cooked and
  coarsely chopped (see
  Chap. XIII)
3 cups bread cubes
½ cup butter
¼ cup celery, chopped
¼ cup onion, chopped
¼ cup raisins
  Parsley
  Sage

Rosemary
Salt and pepper
Wine or broth to moisten

Plump raisins in hot water, drain. Melt butter and cook celery and onion for 5 minutes without browning. Combine all ingredients, toss lightly and season to taste. Moisten if desired with wine or broth.

PRUNE AND APPLE STUFFING

1 quart day old breadcrumbs
2 cups chopped prunes
2 cups peeled and chopped
  tart apples
  Salt

Generous grating fresh nutmeg
Apple juice to moisten

If prunes are not tender and plump, steam them briefly or soak them for a short time—it is not necessary to cook them. Pit and chop the prunes, then combine all ingredients and toss lightly with apple juice to moisten. If appropriate for the meat or bird you are planning to stuff, ½ lb. mild sausage meat, cooked and drained, may be added to this recipe.

WINE STUFFING

1 quart day old breadcrumbs
½ cup melted butter
½ cup dry white wine
8 to 10 sprigs parsley, snipped

½ cup mushrooms, sautéed
  in the butter or ½ cup crisp
  bacon bits, well drained
Thyme and marjoram to taste

Combine all ingredients and toss lightly, seasoning to taste.

Rice Stuffings

Rice for stuffings should be cooked only until barely tender, as it will continue to be cooked during the roasting of the meat or birds. If you do not have a favorite method of producing fluffy rice with each kernel separate, try the method suggested in Chap. XIII.

APRICOT RICE STUFFING

1½ to 2 cups cooked rice
4 tbsps. melted butter
4 tbsps. diced onion
4 tbsps. diced celery
1 cup chopped dried apricots
   Salt and pepper

Grating of fresh nutmeg
1 orange, put through the
   medium blade of the
   food chopper, rind and all
¼ cup brandy or white wine

Cook onion and celery in melted butter for about 5 minutes without browning. Combine with other ingredients and toss lightly but thoroughly to blend.

RICE STUFFING I—*for small birds*

The amounts will vary with the size of the birds, of course. Sauté the bird liver gently in butter with a small amount of minced onion. Chop liver coarsely, add rice, a bit of diced tart apple, and moisten with brandy or white wine. Season to taste with salt and pepper and a grating of nutmeg.

RICE AND RAISIN STUFFING II—*for birds*

1 cup cooked rice
2 tbsps. butter
1 tsp. grated onion
1 tsp. parsley, minced
1 tsp. grated orange rind
2 tbsps. raisins plumped
   in hot water

2 tbsps. slivered almonds
Salt and pepper to taste

Toss all ingredients lightly together, season to taste

SAVORY WILD RICE STUFFING

1 cup raw wild rice	¼ cup onion, chopped
3 cups stock	½ cup butter
½ lb. mushrooms, sliced	Salt
1 cup chopped ham	Marjoram
½ cup celery, diced	Thyme

Cook wild rice in broth about 40 minutes, or until nearly tender. Sauté mushrooms, ham, celery and onion in butter for 5 to 8 minutes. Combine with rice and season to taste.

Forcemeat

VEAL FORCEMEAT—*for stuffing small birds*

¼ lb. veal	4 tbsps. butter
¼ lb. ham	Chopped parsley
1 roll, moistened with white wine	Salt and pepper
1 tbsp. minced onion	1 egg, beaten
1 tbsp. chopped mushroom	

Put veal and ham through the food chopper, using the fine blade. Sauté the mushrooms and onion briefly in butter. Pound all ingredients together until smooth and bind with the egg.

Stuffings for Fish

BREAD STUFFING

¼ cup butter	½ tsp. sage, crumbled
½ onion, chopped	3 or 4 sprigs parsley, chopped
1 stalk celery, chopped	3 to 4 tbsps. milk, water,
2 slices bread, pulled	or lemon juice
into soft crumbs	Salt and pepper
Pinch thyme	

Cook onion and celery in butter for 5 minutes without browning. Add other ingredients, toss lightly and season to taste. Add only enough liquid to moisten—don't let the dressing become soggy!

For variation, you might add: ½ cup chopped mushrooms, or ¼ cup chopped pickle.

CRABMEAT STUFFING

2 tbsps. butter
2 tbsps. lemon juice
1 7-8 oz. can crabmeat, flaked
1½ tsp. finely chopped onion
¼ cup finely chopped celery

2 or 3 tbsps. chopped
  green pepper
Pinch each thyme and nutmeg
⅔ cup fine dry breadcrumbs

Sauté onion and celery lightly but do not brown, add other ingredients and toss lightly to blend.

SHRIMP STUFFING

16 large raw shrimp—
  shelled and deveined
2 tbsps. butter
¼ tsp. salt
  Dash of pepper
1½ tsp. finely chopped onion

¼ cup finely chopped celery
2 sprigs fresh dill, chopped
  or ½ tsp. dill seed
2 tbsps. lime juice
⅔ cup fine dry breadcrumbs

Melt butter, season shrimp with salt and pepper and sauté just until pink and opaque—do not overcook. Remove from pan and chop. In same pan, cook onion and celery for 5 minutes, but do not brown. Add dill, lime juice, chopped shrimp and bread crumbs. Blend with fork.

CHAPTER XI

Nibbles for Party Fare

IT IS NOT CONSIDERED GOOD form to repeat the same food as appetizer and as main course—even though it may appear in a different guise. Therefore, I have included in this chapter a few of our non-game favorites to serve as appetizers when game is to be the featured attraction at a festive dinner.

For evening refreshments or a buffet, let game take the spotlight.

"Non-Game" Appetizers

LIPTAUER

This Viennese cheese spread has as many variations as the cooks who make it. With the exception of the butter and cheese, the other ingredients were added "to taste" and that's the way I've always made it. The taste-testing has always been one of my husband's favorite chores —as a matter of fact, quite a bit of it disappears before he's finished with the "testing." However, we have now standardized the recipe in order to share it with you.

1 8-oz. package cream cheese	2 tsps. caraway seed
½ lb. butter	1 tsp. prepared mustard
½ tsp. salt	1 tbsp. chopped capers
2 tsp. dried minced onion	1 tsp. anchovy paste
1½ tsps. paprika	¼ tsp. freshly ground pepper

Let butter and cream cheese soften at room temperature for ½ hour. Cream the butter and cheese together, add other ingredients and beat until fluffy and well blended. Serve at room temperature on thin rye bread or crackers. It is best to make this at least an hour ahead of time, so the flavors will have a chance to mellow and blend.

(Although I am seldom able to rescue enough to freeze for future use, this spread may be frozen in small containers. It should be beaten again after thawing to restore the proper texture.)

SESAME SEED CHEESE PASTRY

Originally an improvisation in answer to my own question, "What to do with the rest of this pastry?", this has become part of the repertoire. It has always been well received, for all its simplicity.

Toasted sesame seeds	½ recipe for plain pastry
1 cup grated sharp	(using 1 cup flour)
cheddar cheese	

Roll pastry quite thin, spread half the grated cheese on half the pastry. Fold the pastry over the cheese, roll out not quite as thin as the first time, spread the remaining cheese on half the dough, and fold over again. Roll out to about ¼" in thickness, sprinkle liberally with sesame seeds and roll just enough to press the sesame seeds into the pastry. Cut into straws or small fancy shapes with cocktail cutters and bake on ungreased cookie sheets at 425° for 10 minutes. They will puff up almost like a puff paste, and should be served hot from the oven. These can be made weeks ahead of time and stored in the freezer to be baked as needed. For variety, sprinkle the tops with Lawry's seasoned salt instead of the sesame seed.

CHEESE-STUFFED PECANS

About ½ lb. large salted	¼ cup blue cheese
pecan halves	¼ cup cream cheese

Combine the two cheeses thoroughly at room temperature. Place a small amount between pecan halves and press together. Chill for an hour before serving.

CHURAG

This recipe was given me by a neighbor many years ago. I believe it is Armenian in origin, but can't be positive. At any rate, the flavor is unique and delicious.

3 cups flour, sifted
3 tsps. baking powder
3 tbsps. sugar
½ tsp. salt
1 tsp. crushed anise seed

1 tsp. sesame seed
½ cup milk
¼ lb. butter
1 egg plus 1 egg yolk

Sift the dry ingredients together, add the anise and sesame seed. Scald the milk, then add butter and stir until butter is melted. Beat the egg and yolk with a fork and combine with the milk. Add liquid to the dry ingredients and work the resulting dough until thoroughly blended. Roll a small amount of the dough at a time into a long roll, without using any extra flour. Cut into 2″ pieces, shape into crescents and place on buttered baking sheet. Brush with beaten egg and bake at 400° for 15 to 20 minutes, or until delicately browned.

CHEESE-OLIVE PUFFS

2 cups grated sharp
    cheddar cheese
¼ lb. butter
1 cup flour
½ tsp. salt

½ tsp. dry mustard
Dash of cayenne
Small stuffed green olives,
    well drained

Sift dry ingredients together. Work softened butter and cheese together and combine with dry ingredients. Mix thoroughly and wrap a spoon of the cheese mixture around each olive, covering the olive completely. Chill until firm. Just before serving, sprinkle each puff with paprika, and bake on ungreased baking sheet for 15 minutes at 400°. Depending on the size of the olives, this will make 40 to 50 puffs.

SARDINE SPREAD

1 3¾ oz. can sardines, drained
¼ cup butter
1 tsp. prepared mustard

1 tsp. lemon juice
Minced onion to taste

Cream butter, beat in other ingredients and season to taste with onion. May be used as a spread for crackers or toast rounds, or to fill miniature cream puffs.

Shrimp butter may be made in the same way, omitting the mustard, and adding 1 tsp. finely diced celery and 1 tsp. finely diced green pepper.

CHEESE MOUSSE

1 tbsp. unflavored gelatine
¼ cup cold water
½ cup Roquefort cheese
⅓ cup Camembert cheese
1 egg, separated

1 tbsp. sherry
Dash Worcestershire sauce
3 tbsps. chopped parsley
½ cup whipping cream

Soften gelatine in cold water, set in pan of hot water and dissolve completely. In small mixing bowl, cream the two cheeses together with electric beater until well blended. Beat in egg yolk, sherry and Worcestershire sauce. Add dissolved gelatine and blend well. Beat egg white until stiff and fold into cheese mixture, along with chopped parsley. Whip cream in chilled bowl, fold into mixture and spoon into 2 cup mold. Chill until firm—several hours. Unmold onto chilled plate, garnish with pimento and parsley. Surround mold with assorted crackers.

MINIATURE CHEESE PUFFS

¼ cup butter
½ cup boiling water
½ cup flour
½ tsp. salt
  Pinch dry mustard
  Pinch cayenne

⅔ cup grated cheddar cheese
2 eggs

Sift flour, mustard, cayenne and salt together. Bring butter and water to a vigorous boil in saucepan. Dump in flour all at once and beat with wooden spoon until mixture becomes a smooth ball and leaves the side of the pan. Remove from flame, add cheese and beat again until smooth. Add eggs, one at a time, beating vigorously after each addition until the mixture is smooth again. Drop small amounts from the tip of a spoon onto lightly greased baking sheet, bake at 400° 10 to 15 minutes—until golden. Serve hot. (Dough may be wrapped in waxed paper and stored overnight in refrigerator.)

Game Appetizers

BEAVER TAIL

Herewith Mrs. Dalziel's recipe verbatim—the comments are as delightful as the beaver tail is delicious.

"It is a special 'Northern Recipe' enjoyed by most all trappers' families and I have both delighted and astonished some city slicker types with it. It is simple once you know how.

"First you must get acquainted with a beaver hunter, (and don't start thinking of beaver coats) ask him to save the tail from one of his animals. First you thrust the tails into hot coals, or propane flame will do, till the black scaly outer skin puffs and blisters. Use heavy gloves for this or you may blister too. Do this all over. Then, as soon as cool to handle, peel off the outer layer, simple as peeling a banana.

"Wash and put it in a large kettle of cold water, add salt, peppercorns, and a tablespoon of pickling spice, clove of garlic if desired. When tender—only an hour or so—place on platter and serve chilled, sliced—on cocktail crackers—a real conversation piece."

JERKY

The old and time-honored trail food is equally as delicious as a snack or nibble food with drinks. The pioneer method, still used in the bush today, was to cut the meat in thin strips and dry it in the sun and wind on racks over a low smoky fire to keep away insects, removing the water content without actually cooking the meat. The hard blackened strips kept indefinitely and provided a compact and highly nutritious food which could be "chawed" dry, or reconstituted in a stew. Most city folk would find it rather difficult to prepare jerky in this fashion, but with a few "substitutions" you can achieve the same results in your kitchen.

Trim the meat of all fat and gristle and slice as thin as possible with a sharp knife. You are not limited to fresh meat—any of the less tender cuts of venison in your freezer will do very nicely. As I have mentioned before, it is easier to slice the meat while it is still partially frozen. Substitute any of the smoky seasoned salt or herb blends on the market for the smoke of the campfire, adding ground pepper if you wish. Substitute your oven racks for the rack of green willows the pioneers used, and dry in the oven instead of the sun, using the heat from the pilot flame. If you have one of the new ovens with a very low temperature setting for keeping foods warm, (140° to 170°) use that setting, but prop open the oven door, so the meat will be dried without being cooked. If the meat has been sliced thin enough, it will be dry overnight. With most men, I have found, there is no storage problem with jerky—it's gone in a twinkling. If you do have some left over, it will keep well in a tightly closed container—preferably hidden away in a far corner of the cupboard.

MOOSE NOSE

Moose nose, prepared as described in Chap. VII, may be served chilled as is or the meat may be cut in fine dice and jellied. Press the diced meat into a loaf pan or mold, pour over it enough of the cooking liquid to cover—about ½ cup—place a piece of foil on the meat and then weight it. Let it chill in the refrigerator for a day or so, then unmold and slice as described. This is very similar to head-cheese.

PATE IN ASPIC

Aspic:
1 10½ oz. can beef consomme, undiluted

1 tbsp. unflavored gelatine
¼ cup cold water
1 tbsp. Worcestershire sauce

Soften the gelatine in cold water, dissolve in hot consomme and add Worcestershire sauce. Rinse one fancy 3 to 4 cup mold (or several individual ones) with cold water and drain. Pour in a thin layer of aspic and let it get sticky and almost set. Set the remaining aspic aside where it will not gel.

Pâté:
Prepare the liver paste described at the end of Chap. VIII. Shape into a ball slightly smaller than the mold you are using and firm up by setting in the freezer for ½ hour. Place the pate on the sticky layer of gelatine and pour the remainder of the aspic around it. Chill for several hours or overnight, unmold on a chilled plate, garnish with parsley or watercress, and serve with crackers or melba toast.

PARTRIDGE PATE—see Chap. V

ANY OF THE PATES described in Chap. VIII

RABBIT IN ASPIC—see Chap. VI

TURNOVERS—see Chap. VIII—make in miniature and serve hot.

TONGUE ROLLS

Slice deer, moose or elk tongue very thin. Spread with cream cheese which has been beaten with one of the following: chives, horseradish, or mustard to taste. Roll up and chill. Cut each roll into 2 or 3 pieces, depending on the size of the tongue slices. Serve on cocktail picks.

CHAPTER XII

Breads

THERE'S NOTHING MORE HEART-WARMING than the aroma of freshly baked bread. And there's nothing more soul-satisfying than to make it yourself—whether it's a simple type baked over a camp fire or a more complex one baked in your kitchen on a cold wintry day.

A good honest loaf of bread is not difficult to make and is infinitely superior to the "cotton bread" found on so many grocery shelves. Somehow it seems more appropriate, too, to serve the type of breads our ancestors made, especially with game.

The earliest type of bread consisted of nothing more than pulverized grain, salt and water, baked in flat cakes on a hot stone or griddle. This unleavened bread is still being made today in many parts of the world—in Mexico, the tortilla; in India, the chapati; in Scotland, the oat cake or bannock. Here in our own country, the New England Jonny cake had its origin as the Journey cake—a simple bread of ground corn meal and salt that the early traveller could bake as needed by adding water and baking over a fire in the wilderness.

With all the commercially prepared mixes available today, you can produce a bewildering array of breads and cakes by adding milk or water and following the directions on the box. However, the hunter or fisherman who is travelling in the wilds with all his supplies in a pack has no space or need for such things. With a few simple ingredients, he can satisfy his hunger and also his desire for variety in breadstuffs.

Very few men will want to take the time to prepare yeast breads, when hunting and fishing are their primary reasons for being in camp. So let's start with the quick breads and see what can be achieved in the time it takes to get a fire going and the kettle boiling.

Quick Breads

JOURNEY CAKES OR 'PONE

1 cup white or yellow corn meal   1 tbsp. sugar, if desired

1 tsp. salt   1 cup milk or water

While the skillet is heating over a slow part of the fire, mix the dry ingredients together thoroughly, then add the liquid and beat with a spoon until the mixture is smooth. When a drop of water dances in the skillet, you're ready to start baking. Grease the skillet lightly, then drop the batter by the tablespoon into the skillet and flatten slightly with the back of the spoon. When the cakes are brown on one side, turn with a spatula and brown the other side. Good for breakfast with bacon and syrup or jam on the cakes—good for lunch or supper with those freshly caught fish. 24 cakes.

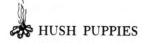

HUSH PUPPIES

Originally, 'pone (as made above) cooked after the fish fry and thrown to the hounds to quiet them—hence, the name. Some hungry soul discovered that they were too good to give to the dogs, so with the addition of two ingredients to the basic recipe, we come up with something slightly different in taste and texture.

3 cups corn meal   4 or 5 tbsp. bacon fat
1 tsp. salt   2 tsps. dried minced onion,
2 tsps. baking powder   if desired
1½ cups water or milk

Blend the dry ingredients together until they're well mixed. Add the liquid and the melted drippings and stir well. Let the mix stand for a few minutes, and then shape into small cakes with floured hands or just drop spoons of the dough into the hot fat with the frying fish, or after it, whichever you prefer. Fry until golden brown.

SKILLET CORN BREAD

A reflector oven of the collapsible type is a handy gadget in camp, but a piece of aluminum foil will serve very nicely to reflect the heat onto the top of such breads as this, so they cook evenly top and bottom. Where every ounce of weight is important, heavy duty foil can serve many useful purposes.

Heat 3 tbsps. bacon drippings in a skillet until very hot—sputtering, but not smoking. In the meantime, measure and mix:

1 cup yellow corn meal   1 tbsp. baking powder
1 cup white flour
2 tbsps. sugar
½ tsp. salt

Take another cup and beat together vigorously with a fork:

1 cup milk   1 egg (fresh or dried and
  (or water and dry milk   reconstituted according
  powder)   to directions)

Add milk and egg to dry ingredients and beat together just until blended. Pour in the hot drippings and beat very quickly and vigorously till they're well mixed. Pour the batter into the hot skillet and set in reflector oven near hot fire until done and golden brown—about 25 to 30 minutes. You can enjoy the same bread at home by baking it in a 425° oven.

CORN MUFFINS OR STICKS

In camp, the skillet corn bread goes mighty well with a big kettle of Brunswick stew—at home, you might like to be just a bit more fancy by using a corn stick pan that turns out little ears of corn bread.
Grease a cast iron corn stick pan and preheat it in a 400° oven. Meanwhile, mix the following ingredients:

3 slices of bacon, diced and fried   4 tbsp. drippings from bacon
    until crisp, then drained
1 cup corn meal
¾ cup flour
4 tsp. baking powder
½ tsp. salt
1 tbsp. sugar
1 egg
1 cup milk

Sift the dry ingredients together, beat the egg with the milk and the drippings. Add the liquid and the crisp bacon crumbles to the dry ingredients and stir just until blended. Spoon into preheated pan, filling each indentation ⅔ full. Bake at 400° for 20 to 25 minutes. If using a regular muffin tin, it is not necessary to preheat it.

CORN MEAL DUMPLINGS

This Roumanian recipe is the "plan ahead" type. You might start this over the embers of your supper fire one evening, and then it's ready for the last minute frying the next night.   .

1 cup corn meal	1 cup grated sharp cheese
4 cups cold water	Cayenne or regular pepper
1½ tsps. salt	

Combine corn meal, water and salt and stir until smooth. Cook in double boiler or over a low fire on direct heat until very thick. Stir it once in a while as you're eating your supper, so it doesn't stick to the bottom of the pan. When the mush is thick, stir in the grated cheese and season highly with pepper. Spread out on a plate which has been rinsed in cold water. When the dough is cool enough to handle without burning your fingers, roll pieces of the dough in small balls and set aside in a cool place until ready to use the next day. Or rinse a loaf pan in cold water and pour the dough into that. When ready to use, slice the loaf. Brown in hot butter or drippings the next day. We enjoy these with kidney stew.

If you omit the cheese and pepper, and pour the plain mush into a loaf pan, you could have fried mush with syrup to go with the bacon next morning.

MUSHROOM SPOON BREAD

If you have a package of dehydrated mushroom soup in your grub box, this is a good supper dish in place of potatoes. The full recipe makes 6 servings, so cut the recipe in half for two people and use the rest of the soup for a mushroom sauce another day.

4 cups milk	1 cup yellow corn meal
1 package dehydrated	2 tbsps. butter or drippings
mushroom soup mix	3 or 4 eggs

Stir soup mix, corn meal and milk together until smooth in top of double boiler (or set a pot into a skillet of hot water). Cook, stirring constantly until thick. Cover and let the mixture steam another 5 minutes. Remove from the heat and add the butter or drippings. Beat the eggs thoroughly in a small bowl and then add slowly to the hot mixture, stirring constantly. Grease a casserole and pour the spoon bread into it. Bake in a hot reflector oven until golden brown—about 1 hour for the full recipe, less for only half the recipe. Test with a clean straw or splinter when the top is brown—if the straw comes out clean, it's time to dig in! If you wish to make this at home, the oven temperature is 400° to 425°.

BANNOCK

As I mentioned earlier, bannock is an unleavened cake of barley or oat meal, mixed to a stiff dough with water or milk, patted out less than an inch thick and baked on the hearth or on a griddle—in much the same way as Journey cake. Since it's quite difficult to find stone ground oat or barley meal these days, I have found the following combination produces equally flavorful results.

½ cup whole wheat flour	½ cup milk or water
½ cup quick-cooking oatmeal	
½ tsp. salt	

Combine the flour, cereal and salt—stir until they are well mixed. Add the liquid to form a stiff dough. Pat out into flat cakes about ½″ to ¾″ thick. Bake on lightly greased griddle or frying pan over a slow fire until brown on one side. Turn over and brown the other side. If you're really travelling light, you could bake the cakes on a hot rock or twist the dough around a peeled birch stick and bake over the coals. Use a splinter to be sure they're cooked through.

BISCUITS

There are so many things that can be made with a basic mix that it would be a wise idea to make up a large batch at home, so you wouldn't have to spend so much time over culinary chores, when you'd rather be hunting or fishing. This mix keeps well in a covered container or heavy duty plastic bag sealed with freezer tape. The following proportions will make about 20 cups of mix.

4 lbs. flour (16 cups)	1½ lbs. vegetable shortening
4 tsps. salt	(3 cups)
½ cup baking powder	2 cups dry milk powder

Sift dry ingredients together several times or mix very well with a spoon to be sure the baking powder and salt are evenly distributed. Cut in the shortening with two knives or a pastry blender until the mix looks like coarse corn meal. When you are ready to use the mix, spoon it lightly into your measuring cup—don't pack it down!

When Chris Klineburger was visiting with us briefly this past winter, we had an interesting discussion about breads. We agreed that we are depriving ourselves of delicious flavor as well as nutrition when we depend entirely upon white flour for baking. The greater part of the minerals and vitamins to be found in wheat are contained in the bran and the germ—both of these are removed in the process of milling white flour. If you can find whole wheat or graham flour in your area, try this same mix with 8 cups white and 8 cups whole wheat flour, increasing the salt to 5 tsps. instead of 4 tsps.

Now on to the baking!

 BISCUITS

Spoon 1 cup of mix into a bowl, add ⅓ cup water and stir until the dough follows the fork around the bowl. Pat out with your floured hand on a clean surface about 1″ thick. This amount will make 4 medium size biscuits for a hungry man, so make up your dough accordingly. Divide into 4 portions per cup of mix used—a knife will do the trick very nicely. Shape with your hands into round biscuits. There is enough shortening in this recipe that you need not grease the pan in which they are baked. Bake in a hot reflector oven 12 to 15 minutes.

For Flavor Variations:

1. Add ¼ cup grated cheese to each cup of mix, blend well with dry ingredients before adding water.
2. Add ½ tsp. of parsley flakes, plus ½ tsp. of one of the following: thyme, marjoram or oregano to dry mix.
3. For breakfast or dessert: pat or roll the dough out to ¼″ thickness on a floured surface, cut 3″ squares, put a spoon of jelly or jam in the middle of each square and then fold over into a triangle, pressing the edges together firmly.
4. Sweet rolls for breakfast: roll dough into an oblong ¼″ thick, spread with butter and sprinkle with brown sugar and raisins, roll up from the long side of the oblong, cut 1″ slices and place close together in

a greased tin. Bake in the reflector oven the same length of time, but watch a bit more closely because of the sugar.

5. For lunch on the run: bake extra biscuits, either plain or with herbs, split and fill with cheese and crisp bacon. Wrap in foil, reheat beside your lunchtime tea fire.

DUMPLINGS FOR STEW

Add 1 tsp. dried parsley flakes and/or ½ tsp. onion flakes to 2 cups mix, stir in ¾ cup water. Thicken stew if necessary before adding dumplings. Dip spoon in hot gravy, then spoon a gob of the dough onto the bubbling liquid (dipping the spoon in the gravy first helps the dough slide off the spoon), repeat this process quickly until the dough is used up. Be sure to leave space between the dumplings when you put them in the kettle—they need room to expand. Clap the lid on the kettle and cook 15 to 20 minutes—no peeking or you'll be eating cannonballs instead of fluffy dumplings!

PANCAKES

2 cups mix
1½ cups water
2 eggs

2 to 3 tbsps. melted butter
or drippings

Beat eggs and water together, add all at once to mix with butter or drippings. Beat thoroughly with fork. Skillet is hot enough when a drop of water will dance on the surface. Drop the batter by the spoonful into the skillet, flip over when bubbles appear on the uncooked surface.

COFFEE CAKE

2 cups mix
2 tbsps. sugar

1 egg
¾ cup water

Add sugar to the dry mix, stir in water and egg which have been beaten together. Spread evenly into greased 8″ or 9″ pan. If you've found any wild blueberries in the vicinity, sprinkle a cup or so on top of the batter, then top with the following crumb mixture:

½ cup sugar (white or brown)   3 or 4 tbsps. butter
½ cup mix   Pinch of cinnamon

Blend these ingredients together with a knife until you have a coarse crumbly mixture. Sprinkle on top of the batter, and bake at a slightly lower heat than for biscuits for about ½ hour. With or without blueberries, it's darn good!

Although the next recipes are not breads to be made in camp, they are old favorites which we have discovered to be good travellers on those weekend jaunts to the wilds. They're old family recipes which Mother used to prepare for Sunday morning breakfast, but we found that a loaf prepared at home and wrapped in foil or plastic will stay fresh and moist for days. The fruit and nuts also provide extra energy, so essential when you're tramping the woods and fields all day.

VERA'S DATE BREAD

1 lb. dates, pitted and cut up   Grated rind and juice
2 tsps. baking soda   of ½ lemon
2 cups very hot water   ½ tsp. vanilla
4 tbsps. shortening   2 eggs, well beaten
¾ tsp. salt   3½ cups flour
1 cup granulated sugar   ½ tsp. baking powder

Sprinkle soda over cut up dates in large mixing bowl, pour the hot water over, add shortening, sugar, salt, lemon and vanilla. Stir to blend and then let it cool. Add eggs and flour sifted with baking powder. The mixture is quite thin. Bake in two greased loaf pans for 1 hour at 325°. During the last 15 minutes, raise the oven temperature to 350°. Turn out of pans and cool on wire rack. Allow to mellow for at least one day before slicing.

ORANGE-RAISIN-NUT BREAD

1 cup raisins, ground through   ¾ cup sugar
    medium blade of food   2¼ cups flour
    chopper   1 tsp. baking powder
1 tsp. baking soda   Pinch of salt

1 cup hot water
Grated rind and juice of 1
orange
1 egg, well beaten

1 tsp. vanilla
½ cup chopped nut meats

Sprinkle soda over the ground raisins, pour over the hot water. Add orange juice and rind and allow to cool. Add beaten egg and sugar, salt, flour and baking powder sifted together. Add vanilla and nut meats, blend well and pour into a greased loaf pan. Bake for 1 hour at 325°, increasing temperature to 350° the last 15 minutes.

Old-Fashioned Yeast Breads

OATMEAL BREAD

1½ cups boiling water
1 cup quick-cooking oatmeal
6 tbsps. shortening
½ cup molasses
1 tbsp. salt

2 packages granulated yeast
½ cup lukewarm water
2 beaten eggs
5½ cups flour

In large mixing bowl, combine boiling water, oatmeal, shortening, molasses and salt. Cool to lukewarm. Meanwhile soften yeast in lukewarm water. Add softened yeast, mix well, then stir in beaten eggs. Sift in flour, beating as you do so. Continue until dough is well blended. Place dough in greased bowl, brush top with melted butter, cover and place in refrigerator for at least two hours. On floured board, shape dough into 2 loaves and place in greased 9″ x 4″ x 3″ loaf pans and cover with a clean towel. Let rise in a warm place until doubled in bulk, about 2 hours. Bake at 375° for 1 hour.

WHOLE WHEAT BREAD

1 package granulated yeast
1 cup warm water
½ cup honey or light molasses
1 tbsp. salt

3 tbsp. shortening
(butter, preferably)
1 cup milk, scalded
4 cups whole wheat flour
2 cups white flour

Soften yeast in warm water. In large mixing bowl, combine honey, salt, butter and scalded milk, stir to melt butter and cool to lukewarm.

Add softened yeast and gradually stir in the flour to form a stiff dough. Turn out on floured board and knead until smooth and satiny—about 10 minutes. Place in greased bowl, cover and let rise in a warm place until doubled—about 2 to 2½ hours. Punch down and turn onto floured board, shape into two loaves and place in 9″ x 5″ x 3″ pans which have been well greased. Cover and let rise in warm place until dough has doubled —about 2 to 2½ hours. Bake at 350° for about an hour—until bread sounds hollow when tapped. Turn out of pans immediately and cool on wire racks.

LIGHT RYE BREAD

1 package granulated yeast
¼ cup warm water
1¾ cups scalded milk
1 tbsp. salt
2 tbsps. butter

2 tbsps. caraway seed
¼ cup dark molasses
3 cups rye flour
2½ to 3 cups white flour

Soften yeast in warm water. Combine in a large mixing bowl hot milk, butter, caraway seed and molasses. Stir to melt butter, allow to cool to lukewarm. Mix in the softened yeast, then gradually stir in the rye flour. Add sufficient white flour to form a stiff dough. Turn out on floured board and knead until smooth and satiny, about 10 minutes. Place in well greased bowl, turning dough in the bowl so the top is greased. Cover and set in a warm place to rise until doubled in bulk— about 1½ hours. Punch dough down, turn over in bowl, cover again and let rise another ½ hour. Turn out on floured board, divide into 2 portions and shape into round loaves. Place on greased baking sheets which have been sprinkled with corn meal. Cover and let rise until light and nearly doubled in size, about 1 hour. Bake at 375° for 45 to 50 minutes, or until loaves sound hollow when tapped. Cool on wire rack.

LIMPA—*Swedish Rye Bread*

1 package granulated yeast
¼ cup warm water
1 tsp. granulated sugar
2 tsps. caraway seed
1 tsp. anise seed
1 tbsp. salt
⅓ cup dark molasses

2 tsps. grated orange rind
   (may be omitted, but we
   prefer to include it)
3 tbsps. shortening
1¾ cups scalded milk
3 cups rye flour
3 cups white flour

Soften yeast in warm water to which the teaspoon of sugar has been added. Combine caraway, anise, salt, molasses, orange rind and shortening in large mixing bowl. Pour over scalded milk and stir until shortening is melted and ingredients well blended, cool to lukewarm. Add softened yeast and mix well. Stir in rye flour thoroughly and add enough white flour to make a stiff dough. Mix thoroughly, then turn out on a floured board and knead until smooth and elastic, about 10 minutes. Place in a greased bowl, turn once to grease top surface, cover and let rise in a warm place until doubled in bulk—about 1½ hours. Punch dough down, turn over in bowl and let rise again for ½ hour. Punch dough down, turn out on floured board, divide into 2 portions, round up into balls, cover and let rest for 10 minutes. Shape into round loaves, place on greased baking sheets, cover and let rise until nearly double in bulk. Bake at 375° 30 to 40 minutes. Cool on wire rack.

MIMI'S HERB BREAD

1 package dry yeast
¼ cup warm water
¾ cup milk, scalded
2 tbsps. sugar
1½ tsps. salt
2 tbsps. shortening

1 well beaten egg
½ tsp. freshly grated nutmeg
1 tsp. crumbled sage
2 tsps. celery seed
3½ cups flour

Soften yeast in warm water. Combine scalded milk, sugar, salt and shortening and cool to lukewarm. Add yeast and mix well. Add egg, nutmeg, sage and celery seed, sift over 2 cups of flour and beat until smooth. Add enough of the remaining flour to make a moderately soft dough. Knead on lightly floured surface until smooth and elastic—about 5 to 8 minutes. Place in a greased bowl, turn once to grease top surface and let rise until double in bulk—about 1½ hours. Punch down, let dough rest covered for 10 to 15 minutes. Shape into a round loaf, place in greased 8″ pie pan. Cover and let rise until almost double—45 to 50 minutes. Bake in 400° oven for 35 to 45 minutes. Slide out on wire rack immediately to cool.

FRENCH BREAD

1 package granulated yeast
2 cups warm water
1 tbsp. salt

5 to 5½ cups flour
1 egg white, slightly beaten
1 tbsp. water

Soften yeast in warm water (¼ cup). Put remainder of warm water and salt in large mixing bowl. Sift and blend in about half the flour, stirring until smooth. Add softened yeast, mix well, and continue adding flour, beating well after each addition until you have a soft dough. Turn onto a floured surface and let the dough rest covered 5 or 10 minutes. Knead until smooth and elastic, place in greased bowl and turn to grease top surface. Cover and let stand in a warm place until doubled in bulk, about 1½ to 2 hours. Punch down with fist and knead lightly for 2 minutes. Divide into 2 portions and let rest covered for 10 minutes. Roll each portion into an oblong and then roll up tightly into a long slender loaf, pinching the ends to seal and rolling gently back and forth with palms of hands to taper the loaf. Place each loaf diagonally on greased baking sheet. With a very sharp knife, cut diagonal gashes ¼″ deep several inches apart along each loaf. Combine egg white and water, brush each loaf with part of the mixture, cover with damp towels and set aside in a warm place to double in bulk. Brush again with egg white when risen. Preheat oven to 425°, place a flat pan in the bottom of the oven and pour boiling water into it. Place the loaves in the oven and bake for 10 minutes. Reduce heat to 375°, brush loaves again with egg white and bake 15 minutes more. Then brush once more with egg white and continue to bake until golden brown, about 20 to 25 minutes.

HARD ROLLS

Follow the above recipe, but shape into round rolls about 2½″ in diameter. Place on greased baking sheets and with very sharp knife, cut 3 gashes ¼″ deep across each roll to form 6 pie-shaped segments. Brush with egg white, cover and let rise until nearly doubled in bulk. Brush again with egg white and sprinkle with poppy seeds. Bake at 425° for about 20 minutes, with a pan of boiling water on the bottom of the oven.

NEW ENGLAND CORN MEAL BREAD

1½ cups boiling water
½ cup cold water
½ cup yellow corn meal
¼ cup molasses
2 tbsps. butter
1½ tsps. salt

1 package granulated yeast
½ cup warm water
6 cups white flour

Combine corn meal and cold water, stir until smooth. Very gradually stir corn meal mixture into boiling water, stirring constantly until well blended. Remove from flame, stir in molasses, butter and salt. Set aside until lukewarm. Meanwhile, soften yeast in warm water for 10 minutes. Stir 1 cup of flour into the lukewarm corn meal mixture and beat until smooth, add softened yeast and mix thoroughly. Gradually beat in enough of the remaining flour to make a soft dough. Turn out on a floured board and let the dough rest for 10 minutes. Knead until smooth and satiny, place in greased bowl and turn once to grease top surface. Cover and set in a warm place until doubled in bulk. Punch down and turn onto floured board. Divide into 2 portions, shape into loaves and place in well greased bread pans. Cover and let rise until nearly doubled, about 1 hour. Bake at 375° for 45 minutes, or until bread sounds hollow when tapped. Turn out on wire racks immediately to cool. Brush tops of loaves with butter for a soft crust.

NEVER FAIL ROLL DOUGH

After years of trial and error, I have finally worked out this recipe which is literally foolproof for light yet rich dinner rolls and coffee cakes. It makes a large quantity of dough, but the lovely part of it is that you can make it all up in one big baking spree or spread the baking over several days.

2 packages granulated yeast	1 tbsp. salt
½ cup warm water	¾ cup butter at room temperature
2 cups milk, scalded	3 eggs
½ cup sugar	7 cups flour

Soften yeast in warm water for 5 minutes. In large mixing bowl, combine scalded milk, sugar and salt. When cooled to lukewarm, sift about 2 cups flour into milk, beating constantly. When batter is smooth, beat in butter in small portions until thoroughly blended. Add yeast, another cup of flour and again beat until smooth. Add eggs, one at a time, beating vigorously after each addition until thoroughly blended. Add remaining flour and beat smooth. Turn into liberally buttered bowl large enough for dough to double (or use 2 smaller bowls) and brush top of dough liberally with melted butter. Cover with waxed paper and towel, set in warm draft-free place until doubled. Punch down with spoon, be sure top surface is completely buttered and refrigerate covered for at least 4 hours and up to 2 days.

This dough is very sticky to work with unless it has been thoroughly chilled. When ready to bake, punch dough down, turn out on lightly floured board and knead gently for a minute or so. Cut off ¼ of the dough, return the remainder to the refrigerator covered. Shape rolls as desired—rosettes, crescents, bow knots, braids. Place on greased baking sheets, brush with melted butter, cover and let rise until almost double. Bake at 400° until golden brown, the time will depend on the size of the rolls.

Sweet rolls and coffee cakes of all sorts may also be made with this dough, baking usually at 350° to 375°.

Note to Busy Housewives: All baked goods freeze well. Cool completely, then wrap tightly in aluminum foil or in plastic bags, excluding all possible air. Keep an extra coffee cake and at least a dozen dinner rolls in the freezer, plus a loaf of home-made bread. Then you can turn the most ordinary meal into something rather special when unexpected guests arrive.

Delicious But Unclassifiable

These two Austrian specialties are among our favorites. The Kartoffelknödel are as essential to Sauerbraten as cheese is to apple pie. The Austrian pancakes are versatile, to say the least, and will often solve the problem of "What to have for supper?"

KARTOFFELKNÖDEL—*Potato Dumplings*

5 medium potatoes	1 or 2 slices of bread, trimmed
4 tbsps. farina	of crusts and cut into cubes
1 egg	2 tbsps. butter
1 tsp. salt	2 quarts boiling water
¾ cup flour	2 tsps. salt
Generous grating of nutmeg	

Boil peeled potatoes in salted water until tender—25 to 30 minutes. Drain and put through ricer, add farina, mix well and let rest for 1 hour. Brown bread cubes lightly in skillet in melted butter over low flame. Add egg, salt and nutmeg to potatoes and beat until fluffy. Add toasted bread cubes and half the flour, mix well. Continue sifting in flour and mixing until you have a soft dough. Shape one 2" dumpling, roll in flour and cook in boiling salted water. If it does not retain its shape, add more flour to the dough. When dough is of right consistency, shape dumplings into 2″ balls, roll lightly in flour and cook in rapidly boiling salted water for 15 minutes, or until dumplings rise to the surface of the water. Do not attempt to cook too many at once, as this will lower the temperature of the water. Drain with a slotted spoon and keep warm in the oven while cooking the remainder of the dumplings. Serve hot with melted butter. Leftover dumplings may be cut in half, sautéed in butter, sprinkled with parsley and served in place of potatoes the next day.

PALATSCHINKEN—*Austrian Pancakes*

1 cup flour	1 cup milk
½ tsp. salt	2 tbsps. butter, melted
3 eggs	

Sift flour and salt together. Beat eggs until very thick, add milk and melted butter, continuing to beat until all is well blended. Combine with sifted dry ingredients and beat smooth. Lightly butter a 5″ or 6″ skillet and heat over a moderate flame. Ladle into the skillet just enough batter to cover the bottom of the skillet, tilting the pan back and forth to spread the batter thin. Cook until the bottom of the pancake is light brown and the top is firm to the touch. Turn with spatula and brown the other side. Transfer to a hot platter and keep warm in the oven as you continue to cook pancakes one at a time. Because of the butter in the mix, it should be unnecessary to butter the skillet after each pancake. To serve:

1. Fill each pancake with cottage cheese and raisins, roll up and sprinkle with cinnamon sugar.
2. Fill each pancake with sardines, sprinkled with a bit of lemon juice, roll up.
3. Fill with Hirschpastete or Hasenpastete (see Chap. VIII), roll up and serve with mushroom sauce (see Chap. X)
4. For dessert pancakes, add ¼ cup sugar when making pancakes and decrease salt to ¼ tsp. Fll with jam or preserves, roll up and sprinkle powdered sugar.
5. For Kaiserschmarren, make dessert pancakes as directed above. Prepare a sauce of: ¾ cup melted butter, ½ cup raisins, ½ cup chopped nuts, 1 tsp. cinnamon, 1 cup sugar. Tear pancakes into bite-size pieces with two forks and mix into the sauce. Serve at once.

The amount given in this recipe makes 18 pancakes, enough for three for a main course, for at least 4 for dessert.

CHAPTER XIII

Vegetables

MEN IN PARTICULAR seem to have an aversion to vegetables—they "only eat 'em because someone says they're good for me"—and my husband used to head the list!

Many cooks of yesteryear cooked vegetables to death and then poured all the goodness down the drain. Today, with frozen vegetables so easily prepared, vegetables get even less attention from the average cook. Just throw them in a pot of water and cook as directed on the package.

However, it is possible to take vegetables out of that "necessary evil" class with very little effort. Especially when you are preparing a gala game dinner, well cooked and attractively served vegetables can add an extra note of festivity.

To my mind, there are several basic rules to be followed. For maximum flavor, cook gently for a minimum of time in a minimum of liquid. Vegetables should be tender-crisp, not soggy. Serve at once for maximum color and vitamin content. Season subtly—but try a variety of seasonings—there are others besides salt and pepper. Serve attractively—sometimes a combination of vegetables cooked or served together will lift the vegetables out of the ordinary. Select your combinations with eye as well as flavor appeal—colorful combinations and simple garnishes add so much.

ASPARAGUS

The first sign of Spring and always most welcome in our house, it deserves to stand alone. Stand the cleaned stalks in a tall deep kettle, with only enough boiling salted water to cover the lower third of the stalks. 8 to 10 minutes should be sufficient to steam the tops and have the tougher bases tender. Lemon butter, buttered crumbs, or a sprinkle of Parmesan cheese over the butter is all that's necessary.

BEANS—GREEN OR WAX

Fresh or frozen, cook in skillet which has a tight fitting lid. Pour in only enough water to cover the bottom of the skillet, add a good chunk of butter, salt. Add vegetable, bring to a boil rapidly, then cook over low flame until vegetables are barely tender—they will steam rather than boil. For variety: pinch of tarragon—a bit of minced onion and fresh snipped dill—a sprinkle of nutmeg—a few crumbled rosemary leaves. Or dress with lemon butter to which you have added a few crushed fennel seeds. With green beans particularly, I like to cut equal amounts of celery and beans in diagonal strips and cook in a small amount of bouillon with butter and a pinch of thyme.

BEETS

Boil in the usual manner, peel and dice—serve hot with butter to which you have added ½ tsp. chopped chives and 2 tsps. chopped watercress.

For Harvard beets, substitute orange juice and grated rind plus 1 tsp. lemon juice for the vinegar.

Shred raw peeled beets, cook in a skillet with butter, salt and pepper plus either a snippet of fresh dill or a pinch of allspice. Simmer covered for about 20 minutes.

BROCCOLI

If stems are particularly thick, split into several lengthwise pieces. Cook in tall kettle only half full of boiling water. Salt the last 5 minutes of cooking—15 minutes should be the total cooking time.

Although traditionally served with lemon butter or hollandaise sauce, try one of the following for variation:
1. ½ cup mayonnaise blended with 1 tbsp. lemon juice and 1 tbsp. prepared horseradish.
2. 1 cup medium white sauce to which has been added ¼ cup grated Parmesan cheese and a sprinkle of dried minced onion.
3. Sour cream with a bit of crumbled dried tarragon.

BRUSSEL SPROUTS

Soak 15 minutes in salt water to drive out any possible insects, drain and rinse in fresh water. Cook 8 to 10 minutes in small amount of salted water, drain.

1. Combine with equal amount of cooked chestnuts in generous amount of butter—simmer over a low flame for several minutes.
2. Dress with lemon butter and fresh dill.
3. Combine with sautéed mushrooms and a sprinkle of caraway seed.
4. Top with buttered crumbs with a dash of lemon juice.

CABBAGE

Cut each head in eighths or shred coarsely. Steam in tightly covered skillet in ¼" bouillon with a lump of butter and a sprinkle of caraway seed, plus salt and pepper, of course. 5 to 8 minutes will be the maximum time.

1. For variation, steam with sliced scallions and diced green pepper.
2. Steam in small amount of salted water, drain and dress with sour cream and bits of crisp bacon, or a rich cream sauce and grated cheddar cheese.

RED CABBAGE WITH APPLE

1 head red cabbage, shredded coarsely
3 tart apples, peeled and chopped
½ cup firmly packed brown sugar
2 allspice berries⎫
3 whole cloves ⎬ tied together in cheesecloth

Cover with boiling salted water and cook loosely covered 8 to 10 minutes, until just barely tender. Drain and toss with 3 or 4 tbsps. butter and an equal amount of vinegar. For variation: follow same recipe as above, but cook tightly covered in 1½ cups red wine instead of water.

CARROTS

1. Julienne strips of carrot and celery (or both cut in diagonal slices) steamed in covered skillet with butter and bouillon, salt and pepper, plus a pinch of either marjoram or fennel.
2. Bake small whole carrots and onions (cut an x in each end of onions) at 350° for about an hour in covered baking dish with a liberal amount of butter and a grating of nutmeg.
3. Carrot ring:

4 cups sliced carrots   1 tsp. minced onion
2 tbsps. butter   Salt and pepper
   Bouillon to cover   3 eggs, well beaten

Cook carrots in butter with bouillon to cover until soft enough to mash. Put through ricer, season to taste, and add well beaten eggs. Pour into well buttered 6 cup ring mold, set in a pan of hot water and bake at 350° for 1 hour. Unmold on heated chop plate and fill center with fresh peas and scallions or green beans and water chestnuts.

4. Shred enough raw carrots to yield 4 cups, place in buttered casserole, sprinkle with ½ cup sherry or white wine, add a dash of salt and nutmeg and dot with butter. Cover and bake at 350° for ½ hour.

CAULIFLOWER

1. Cook whole in boiling salted water 25 to 30 minutes, drain. Serve as the center of attraction on a heated chop plate, with tiny whole carrots, green beans, cooked celery strips arranged in alternate groups around it. Lemon butter with a dash of paprika is all that is needed here.
2. Dress with buttered crumbs and a pinch of basil.
3. Top with a rich cheese sauce.
4. Spike with toasted almonds, pour over browned butter.

CELERY

1. Excellent companion for other vegetables—cook with peas, green beans, brussel sprouts, carrots, fresh lima beans.
2. Capable of standing alone in the finest company, especially when cooked in butter with a small amount of bouillon, salt and pepper and a bit of onion, until tender-crisp.
3. Toss cooked celery with a light cream sauce and snipped parsley or chives.

CHESTNUTS

1 lb. provides 2 cups shelled nut meats and one of the most appropriate vegetables to accompany game.

To shell: gash each chestnut with a sharp knife and place in boiling water for 15 minutes, then remove shell and inner brown skin. It is wise to do only a part of the chestnuts at one time. If you prefer, you may place the gashed nuts in a 450° oven for 20 minutes and then shell.

To cook: cover shelled meats with boiling salted water and simmer until tender, about 15 to 20 minutes, then drain, and serve with brussel sprouts as suggested before or put through a ricer. Beat fluffy with a bit of butter and cream, season to taste with salt and pepper. Reheat if necessary in a double boiler.

CORN

Fresh or frozen, cook only until milk has set—5 to 6 minutes. Our favorite indoor method of cooking corn on the cob is to place a layer of husks in the bottom of a large skillet, add only enough water to cover the bottom, place the ears on the husks and cover with another layer of husks. Cover tightly and steam. Serve with lots of butter, plain or with snipped chives.

Frozen corn is cooked briefly by the skillet method I have described before, adding a bit of chopped onion and green pepper or pimento for color.

Combine cooked corn with a savory cream sauce, fill small parboiled green peppers and heat briefly in the oven. Hollow out medium size ripe tomatoes, drain thoroughly, fill with creamed corn and bake in a hot oven 400° for 15 minutes.

Fritters, good with venison sausage patties and syrup for breakfast or a simple supper:

1 cup flour	1 egg
1 tsp. baking powder	⅔ cup milk
½ tsp. salt	1 to 1½ cups cooked corn
½ tsp. pepper	

Sift dry ingredients together, add egg and milk which have been beaten together, fold in corn. Drop by tablespoon in deep hot fat (375°) cook 3 to 5 minutes, until golden. Or cook in skillet in small amount of fat, turning to brown both sides.

CUCUMBERS

Delicate and delicious as a cooked vegetable. Peel, if young, cut into ½" slices; if quite mature, remove seeds and cut in large dice. Steam in covered skillet in small amount of water with butter, salt and pepper. To gild the lily, add heavy cream, a sprinkle of freshly grated nutmeg and heat thoroughly, but do not allow cream to boil.

ITALIAN VEGETABLE MELANGE

Young zucchini, scrubbed and
   sliced thin without peeling
Frying peppers, sliced
   lengthwise, seeds removed
Sliced onion
Salt and pepper

Garlic salt
Parmesan cheese
Oregano, if you wish

Heat butter or olive oil in large skillet, sauté vegetables over low flame, moving about with spatula or slotted spoon. Add a whiff of garlic salt, salt and pepper, cover and steam for a few minutes until tender-crisp. Sprinkle with Parmesan cheese and oregano, if desired.

LEEKS

The delicate onion flavor is a rare treat. When I do find them in the market, I usually buy a large quantity and freeze them for later use, since they combine well with other vegetables.

Carrots and frozen leeks:

In 8″ skillet, heat ½ cup bouillon and 1 tbsp. butter. Add 4 or 5 whole baby carrots per serving or equivalent in mature carrots sliced diagonally, place frozen leeks on top of carrots, either whole or sliced diagonally to conform with carrots. Cover tightly and simmer on low flame until vegetables are just tender. Season with salt and pepper.

Fresh leeks should be washed very well, as leaves are inclined to be full of grit and sand. Cut off root end and all but a few inches of green leaves. Boil 15 minutes in salted water, drain and serve with lemon butter or a rich cream sauce.

MUSHROOMS

If fresh, it is not necessary to peel them. Saute in butter with salt and pepper for 5 to 10 minutes, depending on whether they are sliced or whole. Chopped parsley, minced onion, a bit of lemon juice or sherry add an extra note of glamour.

BROILED STUFFED MUSHROOMS

Remove the stems from large whole mushrooms, sauté the chopped stems in butter and combine with minced onion, dry breadcrumbs, minced parsley or finely diced celery, salt and pepper. Dip caps in melted butter to coat thoroughly, stuff and broil 5 to 8 minutes. An excellent garnish for venison filet mignon.

FRENCH-FRIED MUSHROOMS

Select large mushrooms which have not opened so the gills are showing. Wash and dry carefully, trim stem end and slice in half lengthwise. Dip in fritter batter (see Corn, this chapter) and then in crumbs. Allow coating to dry for 20 minutes. Deep fry at 375° until golden— serve with lemon wedges.

ONIONS

Boiled in salted water until tender (cut an x in each end to prevent them from separating). Serve with a rich cream sauce, with curry, Parmesan cheese, nutmeg, or sherry. Sour cream with caraway seeds or dill would also be a pleasant variation. Boil small onions until nearly tender, then glaze in a skillet with butter and a bit of sugar until golden.

Tiny whole white onions (or scallions) may be cooked with green vegetables for a pleasing color and flavor combination.

PEAS

Cook in small amount of salted water with butter and one of following: pinch of basil, chervil, marjoram. Celery and/or scallions are good companions in the pot.

Serve fresh peas with cream and chopped mint. Toss fresh buttered peas with mushrooms, water chestnuts or slivered almonds.

RICE

We prefer rice to potatoes, especially with game. Naturally, wild rice heads the list but regular rice can be prepared in many ways that are most delicious.

If you've had difficulty preparing rice so that each kernel is separate and fluffy, try this method which my Mother-in-law taught me. It lends itselt to many variations and is really foolproof. One pound of raw rice (2½ cups) will yield 8 cups of cooked rice, so figure your proportions accordingly. Always allow a bit extra, as leftover rice need present no problem.

Place desired amount of rice in flameproof casserole which has a cover. (Use long grain rice if you can possibly find it.) Wash the rice six times in hot water, then six times in cold water—despite what has been said recently about it not being necessary to wash rice, you will be amazed at how much excess starch is eliminated in this way. Cover the rice with fresh cold water, about ½" over the top of the rice, add salt, bay leaf or any other herb which will blend with the remainder of your dinner, and a generous lump of butter. Place over a brisk flame and bring to a boil, stirring constantly until the water is bubbling and the butter melted and blended through the liquid. Cover and place in a preheated oven—the temperature may vary from 350° to 400°, depending on what is required for the other foods in the oven. (Convenient, isn't it?) After 20 to 35 minutes, test a grain of rice by rolling it between your fingers—if it needs additional cooking and the water has all been absorbed, add a bit more, cover and test after another 10 minutes. When the rice is tender, remove from the oven, set at the back of the stove covered—it will wait until everything else is ready. Fluff with a fork as you place it in the serving dish.

Variations:

1. Use chicken or beef bouillon (depending on the meat or fowl being served) in place of water, add diced raw celery and minced onion, plus snipped parsley before placing in oven.
2. Brown washed and dried rice in generous amount of butter in flameproof casserole. Stir constantly over low flame so that rice does not scorch, but browns evenly. Add sliced onion, curry powder (1½ to 2 tsps.), a pinch of cardamon or allspice during the browning process. Cover with water or stock and proceed as above.
3. Fork in plumped raisins and slivered almonds in butter to the above curried rice for another variation.
4. Add ½ to 1 tsp. crumbled saffron to boiling water or bouillon in base recipe or variation 1. Stir until well blended before placing in oven.
5. For especially attractive service, butter a ring mold or individual custard cups, pack in the cooked rice, cover with foil and keep hot in oven or in pan of hot water until ready to serve. Invert on a

heated platter, fill rice ring with any colorful vegetable, or surround individual molds with an assortment of vegetables for buffet service.

6. Add grated orange rind and 1 tbsp. orange juice concentrate to the base recipe, using a pinch of thyme as the herb.

WILD RICE

This is always the cook's treat when we are having a special game dinner. It's expensive in comparison to regular rice, but worth every penny extra in flavor. Wash the rice well in several changes of water and cook as for regular rice, adding a bit more liquid and butter. Wild rice takes at least 45 to 60 minutes to cook. Add herbs to the cooking liquid—which should be game stock, if possible—or a bit of minced onion. When tender and all liquid absorbed, combine with sautéed mushrooms or slivered almonds and butter. Snip some parsley over the top of the serving dish.

SPINACH

Try this one with moose or elk tongue:

About an hour before serving, set out a package of frozen chopped spinach so it will thaw. Prepare 1 cup of medium white sauce (see Chap. X), add a pinch of dried onion flakes and a grating of nutmeg. Add the thawed spinach, stir over low heat until spinach is well blended with the sauce and heated through. Check the seasoning and serve. In this way, the spinach is not drowned in water or overcooked.

SQUASH

Baked acorn squash is excellent with game, as is whipped squash. This is a nice variation of the latter, for a special occasion.

2½ cups cooked squash	Salt and pepper to taste
2 tbsps. butter	1 tbsp. brown sugar
2 tbsps. grated onion	4 eggs

Beat eggs thoroughly, fold into other ingredients which have been well mixed. Pour into liberally buttered ring mold, bake in a pan of hot water for 1 hour at 350°. Invert on heated platter, fill ring with any green vegetable.

TOMATOES

For a colorful service on the meat platter, or as an addition on a vegetable platter for a buffet, bake tomatoes as suggested under Corn—they may also be filled with peas and tiny onions with a snippet of fresh dill.

CANDIED SWEET POTATOES WITH ORANGE

Good with roast saddle of boar. Cook unpared sweet potatoes until nearly tender. Drain and peel. Prepare the following syrup in a large skillet: 1 cup brown sugar, packed; ¼ cup butter; ½ cup orange juice. Simmer until sugar is melted and syrup is bubbling. Add sliced sweet potatoes and thick slices of unpeeled seedless oranges. Cook over very low flame, turning the potatoes and orange slices occasionally until they are well glazed and completely cooked. Baste once in a while with the syrup.

CHAPTER XIV

Fish

ALTHOUGH THIS IS PRIMARILY a game cook book, many lovers of the outdoors enjoy both hunting and fishing. There are many spots in this country where the hunter packs a fishing rod along wtih his guns and is able to enjoy the best of two worlds on one trip. With others, the fishing rods come out of the closet when the guns are retired for the summer.

In either case, everyone will agree that nothing can compare with fish freshly caught and cooked on the spot. Many's the lunch I've shared with my Dad on Strawberry Island—a Thermos of tea, bread and butter and fish, fresh from Niagara River, sizzling over the campfire. Perhaps it's the fresh air and the thrill of having caught some of the fish yourself that adds extra zest to the meal, but the finest of sea food restaurants just can't compete as far as I'm concerned.

There are times when a larger catch could be brought home to share with family and friends. If you want to preserve that fresh-caught flavor, treat the fish in the same careful manner you do game. Clean them thoroughly and carefully as soon as feasible, remove any excess moisture after the cleaning process and then keep the fish cool. Ice, of course, is fine and dandy as long as the fish are not swimming in the water as the ice melts. Plastic bags are all right, too, as long as they're not punctured. The best combination we've found is Scotch Ice and a portable cooler, but I'm sure you have your own ideas on the subject. The main thing is to be prepared.

Fish may be broiled, fried, baked in a sauce or stuffed, or boiled (although poached is the more correct term)—whatever suits your fancy and the ingredients at hand. There is only one rule to be followed without exception—DO NOT OVERCOOK!!! Even with a large fish to be baked whole, compute your cooking time carefully and have everything else ready, so the meal can be served the minute the fish is done.

Fish rich in fat—striped bass, halibut, mackerel, pompano, salmon, tuna and whitefish—respond well to wine, vinegar or lemon juice when they are baked or broiled. The lean fish are often baked in, or served with, a rich sauce. When broiled, they should be basted frequently to prevent dryness.

It is almost impossible to cover this subject extensively in one chapter. I can only set down a few guidelines and let you take it from there—adding your own personal touches, experimenting and substituting as you wish.

Broiled Fish

BROILED FILETS

Preheat broiler, grease rack or aluminum foil before putting fish in to broil. With filets up to 1″ thick, it is not necessary to turn the filets, so place skin side down on the rack and broil 6 to 10 minutes, basting with melted butter and lemon juice plus seasonings of your choice—dill, marjoram or chives are all good. When the fish is delicately browned and flakes easily with a fork. rush it to the table. You might like to try this variation of the basic recipe:

FILETS WITH A FLAIR

Any fish would be appropriate, but I enjoy snapper, flounder, or bass for this.

2 lbs. fish filets	2 egg whites, stiffly beaten
Salt and pepper	¼ cup toasted, slivered almonds
Melted butter	
½ cup mayonnaise	
1 tbsp. lemon juice	
1 tsp. finely minced onion	
Dash of cayenne	

Broil the filets as described above, seasoning with salt and freshly ground pepper, and basting with melted butter. While the filets are broiling, combine mayonnaise, lemon juice and onion. Fold in stiffly beaten egg whites, spread the topping on the filets as soon as they flake easily. Dust the topping with a light sprinkle of cayenne and top with the almonds. Return to the broiler, about 5″ from the heat, and broil only until the topping is lightly browned and puffy. Watch carefully.

FRESH TUNA FILETS

I have heard many fishermen along the Eastern shore say they found fresh tuna too oily for their taste. A veteran salt water fisherman soon put us wise to the solution with these delectable salt water fish. The oiliness in tuna is concentrated in the dark red meat midway along each side, so after skinning the fish, carefully trim this dark flesh away and discard it or feed it to the dogs. Remove the remaining white flesh the full length of the fish and wrap and freeze the long strips whole (they resemble a boneless pork loin on a good size school tuna). When ready to serve, cut crosswise slices about 1" thick from the thawed fish, broil on buttered foil, basting with equal amounts of melted butter and lime juice. Sprinkle with paprika and serve with lime wedges. If you've never tried lime in place of lemon with the more delicately flavored fish, you've been missing something! (The softer belly flesh on tuna should be poached in court bouillon and used in salads and casseroles.)

BROILED FISH STEAKS

Steaks cut from the round of larger fish are usually cut to 2" thick and should be turned midway in the broiling. 6 to 16 minutes is the maximum, depending on the thickness of the steaks. Fresh salmon, cod or muskellunge are prime examples. Allow one steak per serving, combine equal amounts of butter and lemon or lime juice if fish is lean, less butter if fish is more fat. Broil on greased rack or foil, baste with combined juice and butter, adding marjoram or chervil plus salt and pepper. With thicker steaks, have the broiler 4" rather than the usual 3" from the flame. Serve with cucumber sauce, caper sauce to which chopped hard boiled eggs have been added or dill sauce with sour cream. (see Chap. X)

BROILED WHOLE FISH

Larger fish may be boned and spread flat for broiling or broiled "in the round", as you prefer. In the latter case, a few gashes on the skin will facilitate the cooking. These gashes may be garnished when serving with slivers of lemon or strips of pimento. Pike, bass, bluefish or trout are most attractive cooked this way. Brush with lemon butter or an Italian herb dressing for a change of pace. Turn as soon as the flesh has become opaque and flaky on one side and continue broiling the other, basting as before. You may wish to broil tomatoes and/or mushrooms along with the fish. Here's a slightly different way of broiling whole fish such as flounder.

FLOUNDER A LA JACQUELINE

This recipe was born while we were guests at Montauk for some shark fishing. Our host and my husband did some bay fishing for a change one morning and presented us with "a whole mess of flounder." While we were preparing them for the freezer, I wondered out loud what we could do for variety in preparation. Our hostess mentioned that she had once been served whole flounder stuffed with shrimp—that's all, no details. That casual remark came to mind later in the year and I started "fussing around" in the kitchen. My "experiment" was such a success with the family that I was persuaded to enter it in a cooking contest in our local paper, The Bergen Evening Record, of Hackensack, N.J. To my complete amazement, I was awarded third prize!

6 small whole flounder,   Shrimp stuffing (see Chap. X)
    cleaned and heads removed
Melted butter
Lawry's seasoned salt
Parsley
Lime wedges

Preheat broiler to medium temperature. Enlarge pocket for stuffing with slender boning knife. Prepare shrimp stuffing, reserving 6 whole cooked shrimp for garnish. Stuff pockets (or if whole ones not available, use small filets and place stuffing between 2 filets and skewer.) Place on buttered broiler pan or foil, brush with ½ of melted butter, sprinkle with seasoned salt and broil 3″ from heat until browned and flaky. Turn fish, baste with butter and broil other side, placing reserved shrimp on each portion 1 minute before the fish is done. Remove to heated platter, garnish with parsley and lime wedges.

Fish may be broiled over the coals, of course. Wrap lean fish in bacon strips after they have been seasoned lightly with salt and pepper, skewering the bacon in place with toothpicks. Lay flat on a grill or impale on a peeled sweet wood stick, turning to cook evenly. Watch the bacon drippings so they don't catch fire—a drip pan of foil is helpful in this case.

Fried Fish

This seems to be the favorite method of cooking fish, indoors or over a campfire. You have a great deal of latitude within the basic recipe, as well as in the various sauces and garnishes, so that even fried fish need never become monotonous. Filets, steaks or whole fish are done this way—the cooking time is always brief, but does depend to some extent on the thickness of the fish. DON'T OVERCOOK AND DON'T LET IT WAIT! From the frying pan to the plates, with everything else ready and waiting, including the hungry guests.

Fry or sauté the fish without any adornment or prepare in this way:

Dip the fish into milk, evaporated milk, egg beaten with 2 tbsps. lemon juice or white wine, a thin pancake batter, or a savory bottled salad dressing. Season with salt and pepper. Roll in crumbs such as: dry breadcrumbs with Parmesan cheese or dried herbs blended in, cracker meal, corn meal, any dry cereal, crushed to fine crumbs, crumbled potato chips, or plain flour or biscuit mix (see Chap. XII)

Heat oil, shortening or butter in skillet until hot, but not smoking. If using butter, it should be bubbling but not browned. Sauté quickly over a medium flame until golden on underside (1 or 2 minutes), turn carefully and repeat. Place fish on heated platter, quickly add a dash of lemon to the butter in the pan, stir for a few seconds and pour over the fish. Garnish with olive slices, watercress, parsley, snipped chives or serve with your favorite tartar sauce in lemon cups. There are also a number of sauces mentioned in Chap. X which would be appropriate. If done properly with a minimum of fat in the pan, there should be no greasiness to the fish—just a lovely crisp crust. However, in deep fat frying, fish must be drained thoroughly on paper towels or some such before serving. If you do deep fry, be sure the fat or oil has reached 365° to 370° before you begin. Fry only a small amount of fish at once so the temperature of the fat remains constant. Otherwise, the crust will not be sealed quickly and the greasy results will have you searching for the bicarbonate of soda.

Baked Fish

The recipes listed in this section are interchangeable for various fish, both fresh and salt water. They are intended to serve only as guides for the fat and the lean fish—change and adapt them as you wish—use your own imagination.

BAKED HALIBUT

Suitable also for striped bass, mackerel and whitefish. Marinate fish in lemon juice seasoned with salt and cayenne pepper for 1 to 1½ hours. Place fish in greased baking dish, top with 1 onion, finely minced and dot with 3 to 4 tbsps. butter cut in small pieces. Sprinkle over 2 tbsps. white wine. Bake at 400° to 450° until fish flakes easily. Baste several times with pan juices, adding more white wine and butter if necessary. Transfer with a broad spatula to a heated platter, pour pan juices over the fish and garnish with lemon and parsley or watercress.

FILETS IN CREAM

Pike, muskellunge, flounder or bass filets may be used.

Fish filets
Melted butter
¾ cup cream of celery soup, undiluted
½ cup cream
¼ cup sherry wine
Grated Parmesan or sharp cheddar cheese
Salt and pepper

Place filets in a shallow buttered baking dish. Brush liberally with melted butter, season with salt and pepper. Combine the soup, cream and sherry and pour over the filets. Sprinkle with the cheese and bake for about 30 minutes in a 350° oven.

FILETS IN WINE

Most suited to the fat fish, although most any others could be substituted.

2 lbs. filets
Salt and pepper
4 or 5 thinly sliced scallions, including a bit of the green tops
Several sprigs of snipped parsley
White wine
Soft fresh breadcrumbs
Butter

Place the filets in a buttered baking dish that can go to the table. Sprinkle fish with salt and pepper, scatter parsley and scallions on the filets, and top with a sprinkle of breadcrumbs. Dot each filet with several pieces of butter. Pour in enough white wine to cover the filets about halfway. Bake at 450° until crumbs are browned and fish flakes easily—about 15 to 20 minutes.

BAKED CAPE COD TURKEY

4 to 5 lb. cod, boned if you're
   skillful with the knife
 Salt and pepper
 Lemon juice

Butter
Sage and onion bread stuffing
   or Crab meat stuffing (see
   Chap. X)

Stuff cod and skewer closed, place on buttered foil in baking pan and sprinkle with salt and pepper. Add a dash of lemon juice and dot the cod with bits of butter. Pour in enough water or white wine to barely cover the bottom of the pan. Bake at 350° for 15 minutes per lb., basting several times with the pan juices. Lift from the pan to the platter with the help of the foil and a broad spatula. Garnish with a necklace of parsley and a row of overlapping lemon slices down the length of the fish.

FILETS PIQUANT

1½ lbs. cod or bluefish filets
¼ cup butter
3 sliced onions
 Salt and pepper
½ cup sour cream

2 tsps. grated lemon rind
3 tbsps. lemon juice
   Several sprigs parsley, minced
3 or 4 tbsps. capers

Place filets in buttered baking dish, surround with onions which have been lightly sautéed in butter, season with salt and pepper. Combine sour cream with remaining ingredients and pour over fish. Bake covered at 325° until fish is flaky. The lower temperature is used to prevent the sour cream from separating—therefore, the cooking time will be slightly longer.

STRIPER IN CREOLE SAUCE

4 to 5 lb. striped bass
 Butter
 Salt and pepper

2 cups Creole sauce (see
   Chap. X)
½ cup white wine
   or tomato juice

Place seasoned fish in buttered baking dish. Thin Creole sauce with half of the extra liquid and pour over the fish. Bake at 350° about 35 to 40 minutes, basting the fish several times and adding more of the liquid if the sauce seems too thick.

ALSATIAN FISH PATE

2½ lbs. salmon, pike or trout
1 cup dry white wine
¾ lb. cod
½ cup dry bread crumbs
½ cup finely chopped
   sautéed mushrooms

2 egg yolks, well beaten
1½ tbsps. melted butter
Salt and pepper
Several sprigs of parsley,
   chopped

Bone and skin the salmon, cut in 1" pieces, marinate in white wine for 4 hours, turning once or twice. Chop the cod very fine and blend well with remaining ingredients, seasoning to taste with salt and pepper. Add the wine in which the salmon has been marinating, mixing well. Butter a covered casserole, place in it a layer of salmon, spread over ½ the dressing, add the remainder of the salmon and then the balance of the dressing. Cover and bake at 350° for 45 minutes. Uncover and bake 10 or 15 minutes longer to brown the dressing.

ROLLED STUFFED FILETS

6 thin filets of flounder, or
   any other delicate lean fish
   Shrimp or crab meat stuffing
   (see Chap. X)
½ cup white wine
1 tbsp. lemon juice
   Parmesan Cheese

White wine sauce (see
   Chap. X)
   substituting fish stock for
   game bird stock
Large pieces of crab claw meat
   or whole shrimp for garnish

Season filets with salt and pepper, spread with stuffing and roll up, securing with toothpicks. Place in buttered casserole, pour over wine and lemon juice and bake at 375° until fish is flaky but still moist— about ½ hour. Transfer filets to ovenproof platter, remove toothpicks, pour over warm sauce, sprinkle with Parmesan and garnish with shrimp or crab which has been brushed with butter. Slide under broiler on medium flame for a minute or two until cheese is melted and the sauce slightly browned.

FISH FLORENTINE

1½ to 2 lbs. lean fish filets   Parmesan cheese
    Double recipe of spinach   Salt and pepper
        prepared as directed in   Paprika
        Chap. XIII   Melted butter

Butter a casserole which can go to the table. Spoon in the spinach, place the filets on top. Brush the filets liberally with melted butter, season with salt and pepper. Bake at 375° for 15 minutes, then sprinkle on Parmesan cheese and return to oven until fish flakes easily, probably another 5 to 10 minutes. Sprinkle with paprika before serving.

CAMP BAKED BASS

Grease a shallow pan, place in it seasoned fish, cover with canned tomatoes, sliced onions and a sprinkle of basil or oregano, if you have it along. Place in hot reflector oven and bake until fish flakes easily, basting once in a while with the liquid in the pan. (Trout and perch are also good fixed this way.)

LITTLE BARNDOOR SALMON

Little Barndoor Island on Lake Winnipesaukee, N.H., was the scene of many an outdoor feast. Among my fondest memories is "the day of the land-locked salmon" and Jim Warner's recipe for same. It is, of course, applicable to most any fish. Melt butter in shallow pan, brown sliced onions slowly, place seasoned fish (either whole or in filets) on top of onions, brush top of fish with butter and pour milk around the fish. Place in reflector oven and bake until fish is easily flaked. Baste occasionally with the pan juices.

FISH BAKED IN CLAY

If you have good sticky clay in your camping area, you're in luck. Plaster a good thick layer of the stuff on a whole fish just as it comes from the water. Bury it in the embers of your fire, place more coals on top of the package and let it bake for about 20 minutes per lb. This is no time to fib about how much that fish weighed or it will be overdone! Crack open the hard block, scales and skin will be attached to the hardened clay and the entrails will have shrivelled up. Season the steaming fish and dig in!

Poached Fish

Poaching fish is a most delectable way of preparing it—if done properly. Otherwise, it is disastrous.

Lean fish are usually recommended for poaching since they do not disintegrate as easily as the fatter fleshed ones. There are always exceptions that prove the rule, the most notable in this case being the salmon, followed by the halibut, mackerel, shad and whitefish. Court bouillon, a seasoned broth for poaching fish, is prepared first in a kettle which will accommodate the fish.

Large whole cleaned fish are wrapped in parchment or cheesecloth to help them retain their shape, then placed on a rack with cold court bouillon to cover. The liquid is brought rapidly to the boiling point, skimmed and then simmered *very* slowly, with the liquid barely bubbling, until the fish is done. 6 to 10 minutes per lb., depending on the thickness of the fish, is the general rule.

For small whole fish, slices or filets, the method is slightly different. First of all, the slices or filets must be fairly thick. They are placed on a Pyrex plate or in a wire basket with cheesecloth wrapped around the entire thing, then lowered into *boiling* court bouillon. This is done to seal the outside of the pieces as quickly as possible to prevent loss of flavor and to keep the slices from falling apart. The temperature is then lowered so the water is scarcely bubbling. Slices or filets are poached for 10 to 20 minutes, depending on their thickness.

Hot poached fish is traditionally served with melted butter, hollandaise, a rich cream sauce with chopped hard boiled egg, caper sauce, cucumber sauce. If the fish is to be served cold, allow it to cool in the court bouillon to prevent drying. A cold savory sauce with mayonnaise or sour cream may be used to dress the chilled fish. Add chives, capers, chopped pickle—as you wish.

COURT BOUILLON

2 quarts water and 1/2 cup vinegar or, 1 quart water and 1 cup white wine, 1 tbsp. salt, 2 sliced carrots, 1 large onion, 6 to 8 peppercorns, Bouquet garni: parsley, bay leaf, celery. Combine all ingredients, simmer 30 minutes, and strain.

CHAPTER XV

Man-Pleasers!

When it comes to the question of dessert, the usual response in our house is "Anything, as long as it's chocolate!" Chocolate is fine in its place, but I have "snuck in" a few non-chocolate items along the way that have found enthusiastic acceptance.

Take-Alongs for Short Hunting Trips

FUDGE BROWNIES

This, as I recall, was my first "substitute" recipe. I had started to prepare a double batch of brownies when I discovered that I was short of the necessary amount of white sugar. With my fingers crossed, I substituted brown sugar for 1 cup of the white sugar and have been making them that way ever since. The brown sugar adds flavor and also keeps them from drying out too fast.

½ lb. butter
4 oz. (squares) bitter chocolate
3 eggs
1 cup granulated sugar
1 cup light brown sugar,
   firmly packed

2 tsps. vanilla
1½ cups flour
1 tsp. baking powder
1 tsp. salt
1 8-oz. package walnuts,
   coarsely broken

Melt chocolate and butter together over hot water, then set aside to cool. Beat eggs until thick, add sugars and vanilla, beating until well blended. Continue to beat while adding chocolate. Sift dry ingredients together and mix in thoroughly. Add walnuts and stir in. Spread into jelly roll pan 10″ x 14″ which has been lined with waxed paper. Bake at 350° for 30 minutes, turning pan around in the oven after 20 minutes. Cool, turn out of pan, peel off waxed paper and cut into 4 large squares. Wrap each section in foil and freeze. I prefer not to cut any pan cookies of this type until they are to be eaten—there is less chance of them drying out.

Serving suggestions:

1. Frost with chocolate butter frosting, cut into 1½" squares.
2. Cut large squares, top with scoop of coffee ice cream and chocolate sauce.

Friendly Tip to Wives: Make these when your menfolk aren't around or they'll disappear in a twinkling. Hide them in a corner of the freezer to discourage raiders.

FRUIT BARS

These were originally concocted to use up candied fruit left over from the Christmas baking—they have since been accepted with almost as much enthusiasm as brownies. They are excellent for hunting trips, since they travel well, stay moist and are high in energy.

½ lb. butter	1 tsp. soda
2 cups light brown sugar, firmly packed	1 tsp. cinnamon
	¼ cup milk
2 eggs	¾ cup mixed candied fruit
1½ tsps. vanilla	½ cup nuts, coarsely chopped
3 cups flour	

Cream butter and sugar together, add eggs and beat well. Blend in vanilla. Sift dry ingredients together and add alternately with milk. Blend in fruit and nuts. Spread in waxed paper lined jelly roll pan and bake at 350° for ½ hour, turning pan in the oven after 20 minutes. Cool, package and freeze in the same way as brownies.

BUTTERSCOTCH BROWNIES

1¾ cups flour	1½ cups light brown sugar, firmly packed
½ tsp. baking powder	
¾ tsp. salt	3 eggs
¾ cup butter	1 tsp. vanilla
	2 cups pecans

Sift dry ingredients together. Cream butter and sugar, then add eggs, one at a time, beating well after each addition. Add vanilla, then sifted dry ingredients. Mix thoroughly, then blend in nuts. Spread in waxed paper lined jelly roll pan and bake at 350° for 25 minutes. Cool, package and freeze as above.

FRUIT-FILLED OATMEAL SQUARES

These, too, stay moist and are high in energy. The choice of fillings is endless—I have mentioned a few.

¾ cup butter	½ tsp. salt
1 cup brown sugar, firmly packed	1 tsp. soda
1¾ cups flour	2 cups quick cooking oatmeal

Cream butter and sugar together thoroughly, add dry ingredients which have been sifted together. Mix in oatmeal until the dough is well blended and very crumbly. Line a jelly roll pan with waxed paper and pat ½ of the oatmeal mixture evenly and firmly into the pan. Spread with the fruit filling of your choice, add the remainder of the crumbs and pat down. Bake at 350° for 25 to 30 minutes.

Cook any of the following combinations to the consistency of thick jam:

Raisin: 2½ cups raisins, ½ cup sugar mixed with 2 tbsps. cornstarch, ¾ cup water, ¼ cup lemon juice.

Date: 1 lb. dates, pitted and cut up, ¾ cup white sugar, ½ cup water, ½ cup orange juice, 1 tbsp. lemon juice, coarsely shredded rind of 1 orange.

Apricot: 3 cups chopped dried apricots, ½ cup water, ½ cup orange juice, 1 cup sugar. Add ¾ cup chopped walnuts after cooling the fruit mixture.

Any other thick jam or preserves.

RANGERS

These good travellers have ranged far and wide in this country. Mother always included them in packages of "goodies" mailed to us when we were away at school.

1 cup vegetable shortening	1 tsp. soda
1 cup granulated sugar	½ tsp. baking powder
1 cup light brown sugar, firmly packed	½ tsp. salt
	2 cups quick cooking oats

1 tbsp. milk
2 eggs
1 tsp. vanilla
2 cups flour

1 cup coconut
2 cups corn flakes
½ cup walnuts, coarsely broken

Cream shortening and sugars together, continue to beat as you add milk, eggs and vanilla. Sift dry ingredients together and beat in until well blended. Stir in oats, coconut, corn flakes and nuts. Mix thoroughly. Drop by spoonsful on greased baking sheets and bake at 350° for 9 to 10 minutes, reversing the pans after 5 or 6 minutes in the oven, so all the cookies will brown evenly.

Plan Ahead Hint: Save dishwashing time and prepare a double batch while you have the ingredients out. Bake some of the cookies right away, drop the remainder of the dough by the spoonful on waxed paper covered pans very close together. Freeze uncovered until the cookies are hard, then store unbaked in plastic bags for emergency use. For freshly baked cookies in 15 minutes, preheat oven while you grease a baking sheet. Place the individually frozen cookies on it and into the oven. It will take only a minute or so longer than the normal baking time. You may, of course, freeze the baked cookies but my own preference has always been for cookies fresh from the oven.

Campfire Desserts

These may be made at home as well, but their simplicity makes them ideal for camp cooking.

 BLUEBERRY ROLL

Wild blueberries are available through mid-October in the North country. If you find some in your travels, pick a hat full! Better yet, go back with a pail!

Wash 2 cups blueberries and drain while you prepare the dough. Take 2 cups of the biscuit mix (see Chap. XII) add an extra tbsp. of sugar if you wish, but it isn't really necessary. Mix it just as you would for regular biscuits and roll or pat it out on a clean floured surface to ½" thickness in an oblong shape. Mix the blueberries with ½ cup sugar and sprinkle over 1½ tbsps. lemon juice or reconstituted lemon crystals. Distribute the fruit over the dough, leaving an inch on the short side of the oblong uncovered. Roll up, starting at the opposite short side. Place seam down on greased pan and bake in hot reflector oven for 25 to 30 minutes. Cut in crosswise slices and serve with lemon sauce.

You could also use any dried and stewed fruit, mashed to a pulp with a fork and spread over the dough.

Wild cranberries would also be a treat this way, but add a bit more sugar—they are considerably more tart.

LEMON DESSERT SAUCE

Moisten 1 tbsp. corn starch or 2 tbsps. flour with 2 tbsps. cold water, mix well till you have all the lumps out. Corn starch will give you a clear sauce, flour will not—but who cares, if it tastes good? Now, in a small pan mix the following: ¾ cup water, pinch of salt, ¼ cup sugar, 3 or 4 tbsps. lemon juice or reconstituted crystals (if you don't have lemon, use orange or grapefruit). Bring to a boil, add thickening and stir over low heat until thick. Simmer 5 minutes, remove from the fire and stir in 1 tbsp. butter.

This sauce is good on other desserts, too.

DESSERT PANCAKES

Make up pancake batter as directed in Chap. XII. For each cup of mix used, add ½ cup washed and drained blueberries after the batter is made up. Cook as you would regular pancakes. Eat with butter and brown sugar—or wild honey. If you're a chocolate fiend, you could use chocolate chips, but in this case be sure the pan is well greased.

Raisins or chopped apricots could also be used.

BAKED APPLES

In deer and ruffed grouse country, you're quite likely to stumble upon an abandoned orchard—as a matter of fact, you probably had it spotted long before the season opened. We've found some pretty good apples in these old orchards with a bit of searching.

Core the apples and cut through the skin around the middle of the apple—that's to keep it from bursting as it's cooked. Place each apple on a double square of foil, fill the centers with cinnamon and sugar, brown sugar and raisins, dried mincemeat reconstituted according to package directions. Add a bit of butter to each package, fold over securely with the drugstore wrap. Place beside the coals of your dinner fire, turn once in a while to insure even cooking. Depending on the size of the apples and the heat of the fire, they should be ready in less than an hour.

APPLE CRISP

If the apples you found are not perfect enough for baking whole, this is a good dessert to make using only the good parts of the apples. Butter a baking dish, peel and slice into it enough apples to equal 6 or 7 whole ones. Sprinkle the apples with 2 tbsps. lemon juice and some grated rind if you have it. Top with the following mixed together until crumbly: ¼ cup flour or biscuit mix, ¾ cup brown sugar packed into the cup, a dash of nutmeg or cinnamon, 4 tbsps. butter and ¾ cup dry cereal (corn flakes, rice flakes, etc.). Pat this firmly atop the apples and bake in a moderate reflector oven for 45 minutes. (350° if you want to make it at home.) Serve warm with cream or as is.

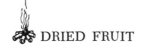

DRIED FRUIT

Although the modern processing makes dried fruit tender enough to eat as is for a quick energy snack, it is somehow more appealing for dessert when it has been cooked for a time. This is our favorite method. Barely cover the fruit with water and set over a slow fire to simmer gently (unless you prefer fruit mush). Add a dash of cinnamon or a piece of stick cinnamon and a few whole cloves. If you have it, slice a lemon in *very* thin slices and simmer it along with the fruit. There is also a dried grated lemon peel on the market now which makes a mighty good substitute. Most people seem to like fruit very sweet—I don't—so sugar to your own taste, preferably after the fruit is cooked and removed. Then boil down the remaining syrup and pour over the fruit.

FRUIT COBBLERS

To my way of thinking, there is no better camper's dessert than the old New England cobbler, for any fruit, fresh or dried, can be used. For several hungry hunters, use 4 cups fresh fruit such as blueberries, sliced apples, a combination of apples and wild cranberries. Mix the fruit with 1 cup of sugar blended with 2 or 3 tbsps. flour, add 1 or 2 tbsps. orange or lemon juice and place in the bottom of a greased baking dish. Top with biscuit mix—2 cups—mixed with a bit more liquid than for regular biscuits. Your aim is a softer dough. Drop this by the spoonful on top of the fruit, leaving spaces between the drop biscuits. Bake in a hot reflector oven until the biscuits are browned and the fruit is bubbling, about ½ hour.

Dried apricots, peaches, dried apples stewed as above and then turned into the baking dish are excellent when fresh fruit is not available. For a zesty change, try combining stewed apples with reconstituted mincemeat—it's delicious!

Tart Desserts

Desserts that are not too rich or sweet are most appropriate after a fish dinner or a hearty main dish. These are equally suitable for a family meal or a special occasion.

LEMON VELVET

Especially good ending for fish or a spaghetti dinner.

2 eggs   ¼ cup lemon juice
½ cup sugar
½ cup white corn syrup
2 cups light cream

Beat eggs until very thick, continue beating as you add sugar gradually. Beat until lemon colored and light, then add corn syrup, cream and lemon juice and mix thoroughly. Freeze firm in refrigerator tray. Set large mixing bowl in freezer to chill thoroughly. Break up the frozen mixture into chunks, turn into chilled bowl and beat until smooth and fluffy with electric beater. Pack quickly into chilled tray or freezer carton and freeze firm. Serve with fresh blueberries or strawberries in season or garnish each serving with one or two frozen strawberries for winter service.

A delicious variation can be made by substituting lime for lemon, adding a bit of grated lime rind and tinting a delicate green with a drop or two of food coloring.

FROZEN STRAWBERRIES FOR DESSERT GARNISH

This comes under the "plan ahead" category. Whenever you find large perfect berries with the hulls on, plan to freeze a few of them in this way. Wash and drain carefully. Dip each berry in fine granulated sugar and place on waxed paper covered pan. Freeze solid, then package the individually frozen berries in small cartons. Do not thaw when serving or they will collapse to a certain extent. They will be edible and delicious by the time the dessert is on the table. A ring of these frozen beauties around a Strawberry Bavarian Cream is particularly festive.

DELUXE BROILED GRAPEFRUIT

Place on each sectioned half grapefruit:
1 heaping tbsp. brown sugar
1 tbsp. Madeira wine
Broil under low flame until sugar melts and grapefruit is delicately browned.

LEMON CAKE PUDDING

One of my childhood favorites, proved by Mother's comment when she wrote out the recipe for me—"Serves 4—3, the way you like to eat it!"

2 eggs, separated   2 tbsps. melted butter
1 tbsp. flour
1 cup milk
1 cup sugar
  Pinch of salt
  Grated rind and juice of
    1 lemon

Blend sugar, flour and salt and add to well beaten egg yolks. Then add lemon juice and rind, butter and milk. Beat well. Fold in stiffly beaten egg whites and bake in buttered baking dish, set in a pan of hot water, at 350° for 40 minutes. Serve warm or chilled. This is a very delicate sponge on top, with a lemon sauce beneath, after it is baked.

ROSY APPLESAUCE

Combine equal parts cranberries, fresh or frozen, and tart apples, quartered but unpeeled. For each quart of combined fruit, add 1 cup sugar, 1 cup water and a piece of stick cinnamon, if desired. Cover and cook on low flame until fruit is tender. Put through food mill. This may be made in large quantities and frozen in quart containers.

WINE JELLY

1 envelope unflavored gelatine
¼ cup cold water
½ cup boiling water
½ cup sugar
¼ cup orange juice

1 tbsp. lemon juice
¾ cup, sherry, port or
    Madeira wine

Soften gelatine in cold water, dissolve in boiling water. Add sugar and stir until dissolved. Add remaining ingredients, mix well and pour into previously wet molds. Chill until set. Garnish with small bunches of grapes "frosted" by brushing with slightly beaten egg white and sprinkled with fine granulated sugar and set to dry.

CRANBERRY SHERBET

We enjoy this particularly in the summer season. That's one reason I always freeze cranberries.

1 quart cranberries
2½ cups water
2 cups sugar
2 *tsps.* unflavored gelatine
    (less than 1 envelope)

½ cup orange juice
½ cup lemon juice

Cook cranberries in water until the skins pop. Put through a food mill, add sugar and gelatine softened in orange juice. Stir over low flame until sugar and gelatine are dissolved. Cool slightly and add lemon juice. Freeze firm, then break into chunks and beat in large well chilled mixing bowl until smooth and fluffy. Work quickly, so the mixture doesn't melt. Pack into chilled plastic containers and freeze. 8 to 10 servings.

APPLESAUCE CAKE

This old-fashioned favorite is so appropriate for a country style supper, with stew as the main dish. I usually double the recipe and bake one part in two loaf pans. Frosted, frozen unwrapped, and then wrapped in foil, they travel well to picnics and such and are defrosted by the time you're ready to eat.

½ cup butter
½ cup light brown sugar,
    firmly packed
1 cup white sugar
2 eggs
1 cup thick unsweetened
    applesauce
2 cups flour
¼ tsp. salt
1 tsp. baking powder
½ tsp. baking soda

1 tsp. cinnamon
½ tsp. cloves
½ tsp. allspice
1 cup raisins
¾ cup walnuts

Cream butter and sugars together, add eggs and beat well. Add applesauce and continue to beat until blended. Sift together all dry ingredients, including spices, then add gradually to the batter. Fold in raisins and walnuts. Turn into well greased 8" or 9" square pan and bake at 350° for 50 to 60 minutes. Top will spring back when touched lightly when the cake is done. Frost with lemon butter frosting.

Special Desserts for Special Occasions

CHEESE CAKE

Crust:
2 cups zwieback crumbs
½ cup sugar

1 tsp. cinnamon
½ cup melted butter

Combine above ingredients and pack into bottom and up the sides of a 9" spring form pan. If you are making plain cheese cake, reserve ¾ cup of the crumb mixture for topping. If you plan to top with glazed berries, use all of the crumbs in the crust.

Filling:

4 eggs

1 cup sugar

⅛ tsp. salt

1½ tbsps. lemon juice

1 cup cream

8 oz. cream cheese

1 lb. cottage cheese

4 tbsps. flour

1½ tsps. lemon rind

Beat eggs with sugar thoroughly until light. Add remaining ingredients in order given with the exception of the lemon rind. Beat until well blended, then force through food mill. Stir in lemon rind and pour into crust. If serving plain, mix reserved crumbs with ¼ cup chopped walnuts and sprinkle over the top. Bake at 350° for 1 hour, turn off oven and open the door. Let the cheese cake cool slowly for another hour this way. Remove to a wire rack to finish cooling, then refrigerate overnight in the pan. To serve, remove the sides of the pan—it is not necessary to remove the bottom.

Cranberry glaze:

2 cups cranberries

¾ cup water

1 cup sugar

1½ tsps. unflavored gelatine

2 tbsps. water

Cook cranberries, water and sugar together until skins pop. Stir in gelatine which has been softened in 2 tbsps. water until the gelatine is dissolved. Refrigerate until the glaze begins to thicken, then spread over the cheese cake from which the sides have been removed. Chill several hours before serving.

Strawberry glaze:

1 quart fresh strawberries

1 tbsp. lemon juice

½ cup sugar

1 tbsp. cornstarch

Wash, hull and drain strawberries, reserving perfect ones for the top of the cheese cake. Crush one cup of the less perfect berries, add lemon juice, sugar and cornstarch. Cook over low heat, stirring constantly until the glaze is thick and clear. Press immediately through a fine sieve to remove pulp and seeds. Set aside to cool. When whole berries are thoroughly dry, gently mix with glaze, then remove each

KONIGSKUCHEN

*This one is guaranteed to make the
calorie counters among your guests
forget all their good resolutions.
Once you have tasted this cake, you'll
understand the reason for its royal name.*

glazed berry with a spoon and set on the cheese cake. Drizzle any remaining glaze over the berries. Chill for an hour or so before serving.

KONIGSKUCHEN

The perfect cake to serve with Viennese coffee—strong black coffee topped with a spoon of sweetened whipped cream.

½ lb. butter
1⅔ cups sugar
9 egg yolks
3 tbsps. lemon juice
2½ cups flour
¾ cup blanched slivered almonds
¾ cup chopped citron
    and lemon peel

⅔ cup currants
¾ cup golden raisins
9 stiffly beaten egg whites

Cream butter and sugar together, add egg yolks one at a time, beating well after each addition, then lemon juice. Mix in flour gradually, then fold in nuts and fruit, stirring until well distributed through the batter. Fold in stiffly beaten egg whites, folding only enough to blend. Grease a 10″ tube pan or turkshead mold of equal capacity thoroughly. Sprinkle in a handful of flour and swirl it around until all parts of the pan are lightly coated with flour. Spoon in the batter and bake at 350° for about 2 hours or until a cake tester comes out clean. Allow to cool for a few minutes on a wire rack, then invert on the rack and remove from the pan. This cake improves with standing and should not be served until the next day. Dust, if desired, with powdered sugar—but it really is gilding the lily.

VIENNESE NUSSTORTE

1⅔ cups powered sugar
6 egg yolks
1 tbsp. lemon juice
2 cups finely ground walnuts
1 cup finely ground almonds,
    unblanched

1 tbsp. ground coffee
6 egg whites stiffly beaten
    with a pinch of salt

Using a rotary type grater, grate or grind the nuts and spoon lightly into a cup to measure. Blend with the coffee and set aside. Prepare 2 8″ layer pans by greasing first with vegetable shortening, then fitting in waxed paper rounds to cover the bottoms of the pans. Cut strips of waxed paper to fit around the sides of the pans. Grease the waxed paper linings lightly but completely, then dust with fine dry bread crumbs so the entire inside of the pans is coated. Actually, this is the most work in the entire cake, but there are no successful short-cuts—I know, for I've tried. Beat egg yolks with lemon juice and sugar until very thick and lemon colored. In a separate bowl, beat egg whites until stiff. Place the egg whites atop the egg yolk mixture, sprinkle ⅓ of the ground nuts on top and begin to fold the whites into the yolks with a few folding strokes. Repeat with another portion of the ground nuts, continuing to fold gently. Do the same with the remainder of the nuts and continue to fold *only* until the batter is blended. Gently turn or spoon batter into the prepared pans and bake at 350° about ½ hour. When the top springs back when touched lightly, the torte layers are done. Cool on wire racks for a minute or so, then invert and remove from pans. Carefully peel off waxed paper so as not to disturb crumb crust. I usually do this much preparation several days before a party and freeze the carefully wrapped layers until an hour or so before my guests are to arrive. Place the bottom layer on your prettiest cake plate, spread with tart orange marmalade (English, if you can find it) and then swirl on whipped cream slightly sweetened with sugar and vanilla. Place the second layer on top and frost the entire cake with whipped cream. This takes one full pint of heavy cream. Decorate the top with perfect walnut halves and chill in the refrigerator. If there's any left after your party, it may be wrapped and frozen.

CRANBERRY BAVARIAN CREAM

4 cups cranberries
½ cup water
½ cup orange juice
2 cups sugar
 Pinch salt
2 tbsps. unflavored gelatine
¼ cup water
¼ cup lemon juice
4 egg whites

1 cup heavy cream, whipped

Cook cranberries in water and orange juice until skins pop. Add 1 cup sugar and stir in. Cook 5 minutes on low heat. Remove from the fire, add salt and gelatine which has been softened in cold water. Stir until dissolved and add lemon juice. Cool until mixture starts to jell. Beat egg whites until soft peaks begin to form, then gradually add the remaining cup of sugar and beat until very stiff. Fold egg whites and whipped cream into cranberry mixture. This is another of my "plan ahead" schemes. This amount will provide enough for 2 1-quart fluted molds, each one serving 6 portions. I divide the mixture into 2 fancy molds which have been rinsed with cold water and drained. When the mixture is frozen, I turn it out on serving plates and decorate with whipped cream and a few whole berries from the spiced cranberry sauce, a few hours before serving. It will keep well in the refrigerator. In summer, I often serve it frozen.

Index

INDEX

HOW
GERALDINE STEINDLER
CAME TO WRITE
A COOKBOOK

The author of this book became a good cook by upbringing and inclination, and a good game cook by marriage.

Her grandfather was a confectioner, an uncle was a caterer and all of her family were good eaters. Geraldine prepared entire dinners quite routinely before she had graduated from high school. When she married an avid and expert hunter, the extension of her talents to game cookery was inevitable.

Gerry says she was engaged to Bob Steindler before she learned "that he was an enthusiastic shooter and hunter." When he suggested that she might become a shooter, she was horrifed. She resisted

Result: the main course of another of her famous game dinners.

The author holds a pronghorn antelope with her .270.

briefly, and then proceeded to become an expert. Her arsenal now consists of shotguns, handguns and several target and hunting rifles. Much of the game on which she perfected her recipes fell to her guns.

Cooking is fun for Gerry. She enjoys trying something different, and she calls her compilation of game recipes a "culi-

nary League of Nations." Many of them came from Bob's mother, who brought her collection of European recipes with her from Austria. She is also happy—and outstandingly qualified—to experiment and to improvise. Many of the dishes in this book are her own creations, and others have been improved by her sure and knowing touch.

Early in their married life, Bob began to boast about her cooking skills, especially with game dishes. Since he is one of the country's better known shooters and gun editors, there were those who believed, and accepted invitations to the Steindler table. Repeat invitations tended to become unnecessary, as guests invited themselves back.

The question, "When are you going to write a game recipe book, Gerry?" was asked regularly. It was inevitable that one day it would be asked by Stoeger Publishing Company. By this time, the Huntsmen's Hostess was genuinely distressed at the almost universal disappointment in game meals—disappointment for which she knew the remedy. So she decided she *would* write a recipe book.

We publish Gerry Steindler's *Game Cookbook* with considerable pride, happy that her husband convinced her, about a dozen years ago, that she should put her recipes in writing! We know you'll be happy, too.